ANNE WILLAN'S
LOOK&COOK

Classic Breads

ANNE WILLAN'S
LOOK&COOK

Classic Breads

DORLING KINDERSLEY
LONDON • NEW YORK • STUTTGART

A DORLING KINDERSLEY BOOK

Created and produced by
CARROLL & BROWN LIMITED
5 Lonsdale Road
London NW6 6RA

Project Editor Valerie Cipollone
Assistant Editors Stella Vayne and Anne Crane

Editorial Consultant Jeni Wright

Art Editor Susan Knight
Designers Alan Watt and Lucy De Rosa

Photographers David Murray and Jules Selmes

Production Wendy Rogers and Amanda Mackie

First published in Great Britain in 1995
by Dorling Kindersley Limited,
9 Henrietta Street, London WC2E 8PS

A CIP catalogue record for this book is available from the
British Library.

ISBN 0-7513-0170-1

Reproduced by Colourscan, Singapore
Printed and bound in Italy by A. Mondadori, Verona

CONTENTS

CLASSIC BREADS

THE LOOK & COOK APPROACH

Welcome to **Classic Breads** and the *Look & Cook* series. These volumes are designed to be the simplest, most informative cookbooks you will ever own. They are the closest I can come to sharing my personal techniques for making my own favourite recipes without actually being with you in the kitchen looking over your shoulder.

EQUIPMENT

Equipment and ingredients often determine whether or not you can make a particular recipe, so *Look & Cook* illustrates everything you need at the beginning of each one. You will see at a glance how long a recipe takes to bake, how many loaves it makes, what the finished bread looks like, and how much preparation can be done ahead. When you start, you will find the preparation and baking organized into steps that are easy to follow. Each stage has its own colour coding and everything is shown in photographs with brief text accompanying each step. You will never be in doubt as to what it is you are doing, why you are doing it, and how it should look.

INGREDIENTS

🍲 MAKES 12   ⏱ WORK TIME 20–25 MINUTES   🍞 BAKING TIME 15–20 MINUTES

I have also included helpful hints and ideas under "Anne Says". These may list an alternative ingredient or piece of equipment, or explain a certain method, or offer some advice on mastering a particular technique. Similarly, if there is a crucial stage in a recipe when things can go astray, I have included some warnings called "Take Care".

Many of the photographs are annotated to pinpoint why certain pieces of equipment work best, and how bread dough should look at the various stages of preparation. Because presentation is so important, a picture of the finished bread with serving suggestions is at the end of each recipe.

Thanks to all this information, you cannot go wrong. I will be with you every step of the way. So please come with me into the kitchen to look, cook, and enjoy some delicious **Classic Breads.**

WHY BREADS?

If you were to study cuisines from around the world, it would be difficult to find any ritual more celebrated than the long-practised science and art of bread baking. No facet of our culinary repertoire is as rich with history as the harvesting of grain and the baking of bread. Bread is baked in infinite variety, and these are just a few of my favourite recipes.

RECIPE CHOICE

Breads are easily divided into two categories: those raised with yeast and those with chemical leaveners. Here I will show you a variety of yeast breads, plain and fancy, ranging from a basic white loaf to festive breads enriched with eggs and butter. You will also learn how to bake quick breads. As their name implies, these cake-like breads are fast and easy to prepare because the yeast is replaced with baking powder, bicarbonate of soda, or a combination of the two.

BASIC YEAST BREADS

Split-Top White Bread: this white bread is enriched with milk, then slashed down the centre to split during baking. An indispensable recipe for novice and veteran bakers alike. *Cinnamon Swirl Bread:* perfect for the breakfast table, white bread is enriched with butter and spiced with a mixture of cinnamon and sugar. *Wholemeal Bread:* honey sweetens a dough made of stone-ground wholemeal flour. It is shaped into two-tiered cottage loaves. *Double Wheat Bread:* bulghur enhances the flavour of a bread that is baked in clay pots. *Sourdough Bread:* sourdough starter ferments for 3–5 days in order to develop its characteristic sour flavour, so plan ahead to enjoy these crusty, slightly tangy loaves. *Sourdough Rolls:* sourdough is shaped into individual rolls that are great for picnic lunches. *Multi-Grain Breakfast Bread:* for this hearty bread, buttermilk softens a combination of wholemeal and white flours, fortified with rolled oats, wheat bran, polenta, and toasted sunflower seeds. *Orange Juice Breakfast Bread:* orange juice flavours a multi-grain loaf that is snipped for a hedgehog finish. *French Baguette:* the dough for these traditional stick-shaped loaves is left to rise three times, developing a chewy, honeycombed crumb, and a full flavour. The crust bakes to a crisp golden brown. *Wheat Ear Baguette (Epi):* baguette loaves are snipped deeply just before baking to resemble ears of wheat. *Seeded Rye Bread:* caraway seeds and rye are a classic combination in a dough that makes a dark, crusty loaf perfect with cooked meats, cheese, and cole slaw. *Horseshoe Rye Bread:* rye stands alone in this variation, shaped into a large horseshoe.

SPECIALITY YEAST BREADS

Dinner Rolls: this egg-enriched dough is easy to twist and roll into a choice of 6 decorative shapes. *Challah:* for this traditional Jewish bread, made for the Sabbath, holidays, and other festive occasions, four strands of dough are plaited, glazed with egg yolk, and sprinkled with poppy seeds – delicious any time. *Kugelhopf with Walnuts, Bacon, and Herbs:* this tender bread from Alsace is flavoured with diced bacon, fresh herbs, and chopped walnuts, and is baked in a traditional fluted mould. *Kugelhopf with Raisins and Almonds:* a dusting of icing sugar hints at the sweet filling of raisins and chopped almonds in this cake-like bread. *Onion and Walnut Crown:* sautéed onion and toasted walnuts add rich flavour to basic white bread. The dough is shaped into a ring, then the top is snipped to fashion a giant crown. *Green and Black Olive Bread:* pungent oil-cured olives, a flavour redolent of Provence, are kneaded into the dough for this rustic bread. *Small Brioches:* eggs and butter give this classic French bread its rich flavour and crumb. Each roll is topped with a "head" and baked in a scalloped mould. *Rich Brioche:* kneading in additional butter makes this dough extra rich. The brioche dough is baked in two large moulds. *Cheese Brioche:* Brie replaces some of the butter in this bread. Rounds of dough are dropped into a loaf tin for a decorative loaf. *Potato-Chive Monkey Bread:* mashed potato makes a loaf with a moist and tender crumb. The chive-studded dough is rolled into small balls, then arranged and baked in a ring mould. An American favourite. *Sour Cream and Dill Potato Bread:* soured cream and dill flavour this hearty potato bread.

Sesame Breadsticks (Grissini Siciliani): thin and crisp, these breadsticks are a great addition to the antipasto table. *Spanish Bread Loaves (Picos):* the same dough is made into miniature loaves and sprinkled with coarse sea salt. *Pesto Garland Bread:* a ring of dough is sliced and fanned to reveal swirls of pesto. *Sun-dried Tomato Spiral:* a gutsy filling of sun-dried tomatoes, garlic, basil, and Parmesan is wrapped within a spiral of dough. *Spiced Lamb Pies:* a Middle-Eastern favourite, flat bread makes a tender shell for a minced lamb filling spiced with garlic, ginger, cumin, and fresh and ground coriander. *Pita Bread:* classic Middle- Eastern pocket bread is flecked with cumin seeds and baked in a very hot oven until it puffs. *Red Onion Confit and Gorgonzola Pizzas:* red onions made sweet by slow cooking and pungent Gorgonzola cheese work well together on these crisp-crusted individual cornmeal pizzas. *Spinach and Ricotta Pizzas:* in the spirit of the red, white, and green, sliced plum tomatoes top ricotta cheese and sautéed spinach. Buon appetito! *Chicago Deep-Dish Pizza:* famous for its thick crust, this pizza is made with fresh tomato sauce, mild Italian sausage, and mozzarella cheese. *Pizza Calabrese:* flavours of the Mediterranean – capers, black olives, and artichoke hearts – feature in these stuffed pizzas. *Focaccia with Rosemary:* olive oil is the key in this spongy Italian flat bread, and rosemary is a classic flavouring. *Focaccia with Sage:* when slashed, this sage-speckled dough bakes to resemble a leaf. *Chocolate Bread:* cocoa powder colours this richly flavoured loaf studded with chunks of bittersweet chocolate. *Chocolate and Orange Rolls:* grated orange zest replaces the cocoa powder, and the dough is shaped into giant rolls. *Aunt Louie's Yule Bread:* tea-soaked currants and sultanas, and candied orange peel are added to a richly spiced dough perfect forthe winter holidays. *Yorkshire Yule Bread:* this bread is spiked with a generous tot of whisky, and baked in a charlotte mould.

QUICK BREADS

Old-Fashioned Cornbread: a cast-iron frying pan gives a crisp golden crust to cornbread studded with whole kernels of sweetcorn. *Corn Muffins with Roasted Red Pepper:* roasted red pepper sweetens cornbread batter baked in a muffin tin. *Irish Soda Bread:* a simple bread of stone-ground wholemeal flour and buttermilk leavened with bicarbonate of soda. *Griddle Cakes:* with the addition of rolled oats and a little more buttermilk, the dough for Irish Soda Bread turns into a batter for cakes cooked on a hot griddle. Delicious with butter and homemade jam. *Skillet Bread:* here, a combination of stone-ground and white flours is used in a dough that is cut into wedges, and cooked to golden brown in a cast-iron frying pan. *Devon Scones:* a light hand is the trick to making these teatime favourites, delicious spread with jam, butter, and clotted cream, if you like. *Chive Scones:* when the quantity of buttermilk is increased, scone dough softens and can be dropped from a spoon onto the baking sheet. These scones are especially good when made with fresh chives. *Currant Scones:* these scones are studded with currants and cut into wedges. *Orange-Courgette Bread:* freshly grated courgettes keep this spiced bread moist. The courgette skin is left on to add specks of colour to the batter, and chopped walnuts add a crunchy texture. *Pumpkin Bread:* pumpkin and spice are a natural combination – great for warming up chilly days. *Banana Bread:* mashed bananas, the riper the better, are a sweet addition to this quick bread baked in miniature loaf tins. Try it spread with cream cheese. *Lemon-Blueberry Muffins:* lots of fresh blueberries and grated lemon zest make these muffins delicious. For extra lemon flavour, they are glazed with lemon juice and sugar. *Lemon-Poppy Seed Muffins:* poppy seeds add flavour and crunch to muffins flavoured with both lemon juice and zest. Sugar is sprinkled on top before baking for a sweet, crispy finish.

EQUIPMENT

Getting your hands wet, as it were, is the beauty of bread making. And as luck would have it, for yeast doughs, your hands are by far the most useful kitchen tool. When mixing and kneading, their warmth helps to activate the yeast even before the dough is left to rise. They are the gauge with which to measure the condition of the dough, helping you judge its progress by how it feels.

A generous work surface for kneading the dough is important, whether made of Formica, wood, or stainless steel. It should be the right height for your extended hands to reach the surface comfortably so that you can knead dough forcefully without straining your back. When making dough and letting it rise, a selection of glass, ceramic, or stainless steel bowls is needed, while a pastry scraper comes in handy for doughs made directly on the work surface.

The final step before baking some loaves is slashing the tops to make ornamental designs. A sharp edge is vital to cut the dough without dragging – a scalpel or single-edged razor blade works well. A very sharp small knife or a chef's knife can also be used, depending on the size of the job at hand. A pair of pointed kitchen scissors can come in handy for snipping the dough, too.

Flat breads and rolls are at their best hot from the oven, but most loaves are best left to cool before slicing. A wire rack allows air to circulate as the bread cools, as well as speeding cooling time and helping a crisp crust to stay that way. A serrated bread knife cuts the neatest slices.

You will need a chef's knife for dividing raw dough and chopping nuts and vegetables, as well as a chopping board, vegetable peeler, cheese grater, and lemon squeezer. Other standard kitchen equipment used for bread making includes a pastry brush for buttering and oiling bowls and glazing unbaked loaves, a rubber spatula for mixing quick bread batter, and a sieve for sifting dry ingredients. Saucepans and frying pans are used to heat liquids and prepare several of the fillings.

SPECIALITY MOULDS

There are countless possibilities for varying the shape and size of a loaf of bread, some of which require specialized equipment. A number of breads are shaped in moulds such as a miniature, medium, or large loaf tin, a muffin tin, a soufflé dish, or even a clay flower pot. Speciality moulds include small scalloped moulds for Small Brioches, and larger scalloped moulds for Rich Brioche, a bucket-shaped charlotte mould for Yorkshire Yule Bread, a fluted kugelhopf mould for Kugelhopf with Raisins and Almonds, a baguette frame for French Baguette, a ring mould for Potato-Chive Monkey Bread, a Swiss roll tin for Focaccia with Rosemary, a cast-iron frying pan for Old-Fashioned Cornbread and Skillet Bread, and a deep-dish pizza pan for Chicago Deep-Dish Pizza. For free-form loaves and pizzas, baking sheets are essential. Wherever possible, substitutions for speciality moulds are given – for instance, instead of using a ring mould to bake Potato-Chive Monkey Bread, a round cake tin and ramekin can also be used. In the case of Kugelhopf with Walnuts, Bacon, and Herbs, a ring mould can be used in place of the traditional kugelhopf mould, but it does not produce a bread as nicely shaped.

MACHINES AND BREADS

Yeast doughs can be mixed and kneaded in just a few minutes with the help of a heavy-duty electric mixer fitted with paddle and dough hook attachments, or a food processor. It is important to use a table-top mixer with a fixed bowl as mixing and kneading some doughs is quite strenuous work, and can strain the motors of less powerful models. First, the paddle attachment is used to combine the liquid ingredients. Once the flour is added, the dough hook is put in place for kneading. As far as food processors are concerned, those fitted with a steel blade are suitable for kneading doughs made with small quantities of flour, while a plastic dough blade should be used for those doughs made with large quantities of flour. The use of these machines is explained in detailed "how-to" boxes.

The newest bread-making appliance is the bread machine, which makes, kneads, and bakes bread dough for you. More advanced models even have a timer so that you can wake up to the aroma of freshly baked bread. To give the loaf a more personal touch, you can take the dough out of the machine after kneading, then shape it as you like and bake it in your own oven. Some of the recipes in this volume can be adapted for preparation in the bread machine; be sure to follow the manufacturer's instructions.

SPLIT-TOP WHITE BREAD

🍽️ MAKES 2 MEDIUM LOAVES ⌣ WORK TIME 40–50 MINUTES* ♨️ BAKING TIME 35–40 MINUTES

EQUIPMENT

chef's knife

scalpel†

pastry brush

saucepan

bowls

tea towels

two 20 x 10 x 5 cm
(8 x 4 x 2 inch) loaf tins

wire rack

†small knife can also be used

ANNE SAYS
"You can make and knead the dough in a heavy-duty electric mixer fitted with a dough hook."

This basic white bread, a staple recipe for novice and practised bakers alike, is made with strong flour, milk, and a yeast and flour sponge – a fermented batter that adds characteristic flavour and improves the texture of plain yeast-risen breads. The finished loaves are rich in flavour, and have an even, tender crumb.

GETTING AHEAD
White loaves are best on the day of baking, but can be tightly wrapped and kept for 1–2 days, or they can be frozen. The dough can also be made, kneaded, and left in the refrigerator to rise overnight. Shape the loaves, let them come to room temperature, then bake as directed.
*plus 30–60 minutes fermenting time for the sponge and 1 3/4–2 1/4 hours rising time

metric	SHOPPING LIST	imperial
500 ml	milk, more for glaze	16 fl oz
750 g	unbleached strong white flour, more if needed	1 1/2 lb
15 ml	salt	1 tbsp
	butter for bowl and loaf tins	
	For the sponge	
12.5 ml	dried yeast, or 15 g (1/2 oz) fresh yeast	2 1/2 tsp
250 ml	lukewarm water	8 fl oz
125 g	unbleached strong white flour, more for sprinkling	4 oz

INGREDIENTS

unbleached
strong white flour

milk

butter

dried yeast

ORDER OF WORK

1 PREPARE THE
SPONGE AND MAKE
THE DOUGH

2 KNEAD THE DOUGH
AND LET IT RISE

3 SHAPE THE LOAVES

4 GLAZE AND BAKE
THE LOAVES

1 Prepare the Sponge and Make the Dough

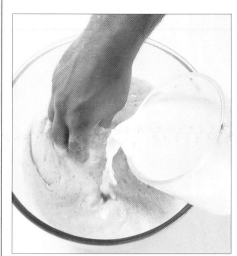

Handle dough firmly

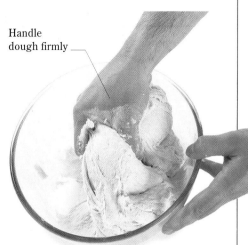

1 Prepare the sponge (see box, below). Meanwhile, bring the milk just to a boil, and let cool to lukewarm. When the sponge has risen, add the milk and mix with your hand.

2 Stir in half of the flour, and the salt, and mix well with your hand. Add the remaining flour, 125 g (4 oz) at a time, mixing well after each addition.

3 Keep adding flour until the dough pulls away from the side of the bowl in a ball. It should be soft and slightly sticky.

How to Make a Sponge

The flavour and texture of bread, particularly plain loaves, is improved when the yeast first ferments in a sponge – a soft batter which froths and bubbles when the yeast starts to grow. The sponge is then mixed with the remaining ingredients to form a dough. The slower the sponge ferments, the more flavour it will have.

1 In a small bowl, sprinkle or crumble the yeast over 60 ml (4 tbsp) of the water. Let stand until dissolved, stirring once, about 5 minutes.

2 Put the dissolved yeast and remaining water into a large bowl. Stir in the flour and mix vigorously with your hand, 30–60 seconds.

3 Sprinkle the sponge with about 30 ml (2 tbsp) flour, covering most but not all of the surface.

4 Cover the bowl with a damp tea towel and let the sponge ferment in a warm place until the bubbles break through the flour, 30–60 minutes. Use the sponge as directed in the recipe.

11

2 KNEAD THE DOUGH AND LET IT RISE

Kneading develops gluten, helping dough to rise

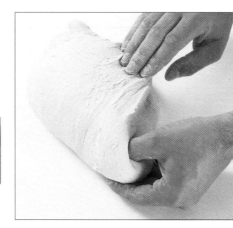

1 Turn the dough onto a floured work surface. Sprinkle the dough and your hands with flour, and begin to knead by holding the dough with one hand and pushing it away from you with the other.

2 Continue to knead by peeling the dough from the surface. Give the dough a quarter turn, and knead until it is very smooth, elastic, and forms a ball, 8–10 minutes. If the dough sticks while kneading, flour the work surface.

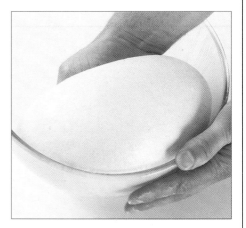

3 Wash the large bowl and brush it with melted butter. Put the kneaded dough in the bowl, and flip it so the surface is lightly buttered. Cover the bowl with a damp tea towel and let the dough rise in a warm place until doubled in bulk, 1–1 1/2 hours.

3 SHAPE THE LOAVES

1 Brush the loaf tins with melted butter. Turn the dough onto a lightly floured work surface and knead with your hand just to knock out the air, 15–20 seconds. Cover the dough, and let rest, about 5 minutes.

2 Cut the dough in half. Cover 1 piece while shaping the other. Flour your hands and pat 1 piece of the dough into a 25 x 20 cm (10 x 8 inch) rectangle.

Roll out dough gently or it will flatten

3 Starting with a long side, roll the rectangle into a cylinder, pinching and sealing it with your fingers as you go. Roll the cylinder until it is about 40 cm (16 inches) long. With the cylinder seam-side up, fold the ends over, making it the length of the tin.

4 Drop the loaf, seam-side down, into 1 of the prepared tins. Repeat to shape the remaining dough. Cover the tins with a dry tea towel, and let the loaves rise in a warm place until the tins are just full, about 45 minutes.

4 GLAZE AND BAKE THE LOAVES

1 Heat the oven to 220°C (425°F, Gas 7). Brush the loaves with milk. With the scalpel, make a slash, about 1.25 cm (½ inch) deep, in each loaf.

Use very sharp edge to slash

2 Bake the loaves in the heated oven, 20 minutes. Lower the heat to 190°C (375°F, Gas 5) and continue baking until well browned, 15–20 minutes longer. Remove the loaves from the tins. Turn them over and tap the bottoms with your knuckles. The bread should sound hollow and the sides should feel crisp when pressed. Let the loaves cool completely.

¶◎¶ TO SERVE
Serve the bread sliced and spread with butter. A full-flavoured white loaf makes satisfying sandwiches.

CINNAMON SWIRL BREAD
When plain white dough is rolled with cinnamon and sugar, each slice reveals a dark swirl of spice.

1 Make and knead the dough, and let it rise as directed in the main recipe. Brush 2 loaf tins with melted butter. In a small bowl, combine 15 ml (1 tbsp) ground cinnamon with 100 g (3¼ oz) sugar. Set 10 ml (2 tsp) of the mixture aside for the glaze. Melt 45 g (1½ oz) unsalted butter in a small saucepan and let cool.
2 Knock the air out of the dough, and let rest as directed. Cut the dough in half, and cover 1 piece while shaping the other.
3 Roll the dough into a 30 x 20 cm (12 x 8 inch) rectangle. Brush the rectangle with some of the melted butter, and sprinkle with half of the cinnamon and sugar mixture. Starting with a short end, roll the rectangle into a cylinder and pinch the seam and ends to seal them. Drop the loaf, seam-side down, into 1 of the prepared tins. Repeat to shape the remaining dough.
4 Cover the loaves, and let rise as directed. Do not let the loaves rise longer than directed, or the cinnamon swirl may separate.
5 Heat the oven to 220°C (425°F, Gas 7). Brush each loaf with more melted butter, sprinkle with the remaining cinnamon and sugar, and bake as directed. Unmould and let cool slightly. Serve warm or toasted.

WHOLEMEAL BREAD

🍽️ MAKES 2 MEDIUM LOAVES   🥣 WORK TIME 35–40 MINUTES*   ♨️ BAKING TIME 40–45 MINUTES

EQUIPMENT

chef's knife

pastry brush

bowls

tea towels

wire rack

small saucepan

baking sheet

INGREDIENTS

stone-ground strong wholemeal flour

unbleached strong white flour

honey

unsalted butter

dried yeast

The finest wholemeal bread is made with a high proportion of stone-ground flour. Stone-ground wholemeal flour varies from mill to mill and batch to batch so you will want to experiment with this recipe, using various flours and adding more or less water. I like to shape wholemeal dough into round cottage loaves. Other two-tiered loaves, that were oblong in shape, were once known in London as "cottage bricks".

GETTING AHEAD

Wholemeal Bread is best on the day of baking, but can be tightly wrapped and kept for 2–3 days, or it can be frozen.

*plus 1³/₄–2 ¹/₄ hours rising time

ANNE SAYS

"You can make and knead the dough in a heavy-duty electric mixer fitted with a dough hook. Instead of making cottage loaves, you can bake the dough in two 23 x 13 x 7.5 cm (9 x 5 x 3 inch) loaf tins."

metric	SHOPPING LIST	imperial
60 g	unsalted butter, more for bowl and baking sheet	2 oz
45 ml	honey	3 tbsp
500 ml	lukewarm water	16 fl oz
15 ml	dried yeast, or 20 g (²/₃ oz) fresh yeast	1 tbsp
15 ml	salt	1 tbsp
125 g	unbleached strong white flour, more if needed	4 oz
625 g	stone-ground strong wholemeal flour	1¹/₄ lb

ORDER OF WORK

1 MAKE AND KNEAD THE DOUGH, AND LET IT RISE

2 SHAPE AND BAKE THE LOAVES

1 MAKE AND KNEAD THE DOUGH, AND LET IT RISE

1 Melt the butter in the saucepan. Stir 15 ml (1 tbsp) of the honey and 60 ml (4 tbsp) of the water in a small bowl until mixed.

2 Sprinkle or crumble the yeast over the honey and water mixture and let stand until dissolved, stirring once, about 5 minutes.

3 Put the melted butter, remaining honey and water, dissolved yeast, and salt into a large bowl. Stir in the white flour with half of the wholemeal flour, and mix with your hand.

4 Add the remaining wholemeal flour, 125 g (4 oz) at a time, mixing well after each addition. Keep adding wholemeal flour until the dough pulls away from the side of the bowl in a ball. It should be soft and slightly sticky.

Hand is best tool for mixing in flour

Dough stiffens as flour is absorbed

5 Turn the dough onto a floured work surface. Sprinkle it with white flour, and begin to knead by holding the dough with one hand and pushing it away from you with the other.

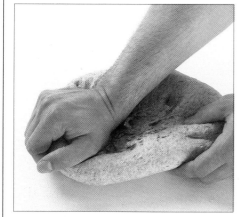

6 Continue to knead by peeling the dough from the surface. Give the dough a quarter turn, and knead until it is very smooth, elastic, and forms a ball, 8–10 minutes. If the dough sticks while kneading, flour the work surface.

7 Wash the large bowl and brush it with melted butter. Put the kneaded dough in the bowl, and flip it so the surface is lightly buttered. Cover the bowl with a damp tea towel and let the dough rise in a warm place until doubled in bulk, 1–1½ hours.

Light coating of melted butter keeps dough moist

2 SHAPE AND BAKE THE LOAVES

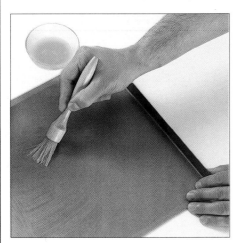

1 Once the dough has doubled in bulk, brush the baking sheet with melted butter.

2 Turn the dough onto a lightly floured work surface and knead with your hand just to knock out the air, 15–20 seconds. Cover the dough, and let rest, about 5 minutes.

3 With the chef's knife, cut the dough into 3 equal pieces. Cut 1 piece in half. Cover 1 large and 1 small piece of dough with a tea towel while shaping the others.

Cut straight down through dough to prevent it sticking to knife

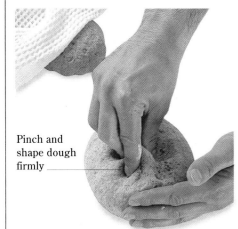

Pinch and shape dough firmly

4 Shape 1 large piece of dough into a loose ball. Fold the sides over to the centre, turning and pinching to make a tight round ball. Flip the ball, seam-side down, onto the prepared baking sheet.

5 Shape 1 small piece of dough into a ball. Fold the sides over to the centre, turning and pinching to make a tight round ball. Set it, seam-side down, on top of the first ball.

6 Holding your forefinger vertically, press through the centre of the 2 balls down to the bottom of the baking sheet and rotate your finger to enlarge the hole slightly. Repeat to shape the remaining 2 balls of dough.

7 Cover the loaves with a dry tea towel, and let rise in a warm place until doubled in bulk, about 45 minutes.

Cover dough to prevent it drying out

Impression made in rounds holds loaf together

8 Heat the oven to 190°C (375°F, Gas 5). Bake the loaves in the heated oven until well browned, 40–45 minutes. Turn the loaves over and tap the bottoms with your knuckles. The bread should sound hollow and the sides should feel crisp when pressed. Transfer the loaves to the wire rack and let cool completely.

🍽 **TO SERVE**
Serve wholemeal bread plain or toasted, with cold beef and horseradish sauce or smoked salmon and cream cheese.

Cottage loaf is cut into thick slices for serving

V A R I A T I O N
DOUBLE WHEAT BREAD

Bulghur, wheat kernels that have been steamed, dried, and crushed, adds extra wheat flavour to wholemeal bread. The dough is baked in flower pots.

1 Put 125 g (4 oz) bulghur in a bowl and cover with cold water. Let soak, about 30 minutes. Drain, pressing to extract any excess water.

2 Melt the butter and dissolve the yeast as directed in the main recipe. Put the bulghur in a large bowl. Add the melted butter, remaining honey and water, dissolved yeast, and salt. Stir in the white and stone-ground wholemeal flours as directed. Knead the dough, and let rise as directed.

3 Heat the oven to 150°C (300°F, Gas 2). Soak 2 clean 750 ml (1¼ pint) clay flower pots in water, 5 minutes; put in the heated oven to dry. Repeat this process twice.

4 Knock the air out of the dough and let rest. Cut it in half, and shape each piece into a ball. Drop the dough into the prepared flower pots, cover, and let rise in a warm place until the pots are just full, about 45 minutes. Heat the oven to 190°C (375°F, Gas 5). Bake as directed. Remove the loaves from the pots. The bread should sound hollow when the bottoms are tapped and the sides should feel crisp when pressed. Let cool.

ANNE SAYS
"*Ask at your local garden centre for untreated clay flower pots, as some can be toxic. Alternatively, bake the bread in two 500 g (1 lb) coffee tins. Line each tin with buttered greaseproof paper, extending 5 cm (2 inches) above the rim to form a collar.*"

SOURDOUGH BREAD

🍽 MAKES 2 MEDIUM LOAVES   🥣 WORK TIME 45–50 MINUTES*   ♨ BAKING TIME 40–45 MINUTES

EQUIPMENT

bowls,

large glass jar, with lid

roasting tin

2 pieces of smooth cotton cloth†

tea towels

wire rack

chef's knife

pastry brush

ladle

scalpel‡

wooden spoon

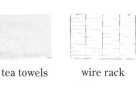

2 baking sheets

†linen can also be used

‡small knife can also be used

ANNE SAYS
"Bakers use bannetons, *round, linen-lined baskets, to hold the shape of soft, wet doughs like sourdough, which tend to spread as they rise. These baskets are difficult to find, so I suggest using round bowls lined with pieces of smooth cotton cloth."*

San Francisco is famous for bread made with a sourdough starter. Authentic starter is made with a flour and water paste which is left to ferment in the hope of capturing wild airborne yeast. This method can be unreliable, so I add some yeast to the starter to encourage fermentation, and to the dough so that it rises evenly.

GETTING AHEAD

Sourdough starter must be made 3–5 days ahead, and the sponge at least 5–8 hours ahead or overnight.
plus 4–6 days fermenting time for starter and sponge and 2–2 1/2 hours rising time

metric	SHOPPING LIST	imperial
7.5 ml	dried yeast, or 10 g (1/3 oz) fresh yeast	1 1/2 tsp
60 ml	lukewarm water	4 tbsp
375 g	unbleached strong white flour, more for bowls	12 oz
15 ml	salt	1 tbsp
	vegetable oil for bowl	
	polenta (fine yellow cornmeal) for baking sheet	
	ice cubes	
	For the sourdough starter	
15 ml	dried yeast, or 20 g (2/3 oz) fresh yeast	1 tbsp
500 ml	lukewarm water	16 fl oz
250 g	unbleached strong white flour	8 oz
	For the sponge	
250 ml	lukewarm water	8 fl oz
250 g	unbleached strong white flour, more for sprinkling sponge	8 oz

INGREDIENTS

unbleached strong white flour

vegetable oil

dried yeast

polenta

ANNE SAYS
"Sourdough bread is best on the day of baking, but can be tightly wrapped and kept for 2–3 days, or it can be frozen."

ORDER OF WORK

1   MAKE THE SOURDOUGH STARTER AND THE SPONGE

2   MAKE AND KNEAD THE DOUGH, AND LET IT RISE

3   SHAPE AND BAKE THE LOAVES

1 MAKE THE SOURDOUGH STARTER AND THE SPONGE

1 Make the sourdough starter (see box, below). Make the sponge: pour the water into a large bowl and spoon in 250 ml (8 fl oz) sourdough starter. Stir in the flour and mix vigorously with your hand, 30–60 seconds.

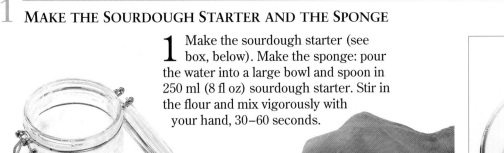

ANNE SAYS
"Remember to replenish the starter after each use."

Remaining starter is kept in jar for future use

Fermented sourdough starter is thick and foamy

2 Sprinkle the sponge with 45 ml (3 tbsp) flour, cover the bowl with a damp tea towel, and let ferment in a warm place, 5–8 hours or overnight.

ANNE SAYS
"If you prefer a more sour flavour, let the sponge ferment overnight."

HOW TO MAKE SOURDOUGH STARTER

This starter can be used within 3–5 days of making. If you don't make sourdough bread frequently, every 2 or 3 weeks stir down the starter to knock out the air, discard half, and replenish it. Let the starter ferment for 1 day at room temperature, then use or refrigerate as directed below. With proper care, the starter will last indefinitely. Discard it if mould appears, or if it gives off a bad, rather than sour, yeasty odour.

Large jar is needed for starter as it ferments

Wooden spoon knocks air out of starter

3 Stir down the starter to knock out the air, cover, and let ferment, stirring it each day, 2–4 days longer. Use or refrigerate the starter.

2 Stir in the flour, cover, and let the starter ferment in a warm place, 24 hours. The starter should become frothy and have a distinct, sour odour.

! TAKE CARE !
While the starter ferments, it is important to maintain an even temperature. Keep the jar of starter away from draughts and high heat.

1 In a large glass jar, sprinkle or crumble the yeast over the water. Let stand until dissolved, stirring once, about 5 minutes.

ANNE SAYS
"To keep the starter active and healthy, replenish it after each use. If a recipe calls for 250 ml (8 fl oz) starter, use it as directed. Then, stir 125 g (4 oz) flour and 250 ml (8 fl oz) water back into the jar of starter."

2 MAKE AND KNEAD THE DOUGH, AND LET IT RISE

1 In a small bowl, sprinkle the yeast over the water. Let stand until dissolved, about 5 minutes. Add to the sponge and mix with your hand.

2 Stir in half of the flour, and the salt, and mix well with your hand. Add the remaining flour, 60 g (2 oz) at a time, mixing well after each addition. Keep adding flour until the dough pulls away from the side of the bowl in a ball. It should be soft and slightly sticky.

3 Turn the dough onto a floured work surface. Sprinkle the dough and your hands with flour, and begin to knead by holding the dough with one hand and pushing it away from you with the other. Continue to knead by peeling the dough from the surface. Give the dough a quarter turn, and knead until it is very smooth, elastic, and forms a ball, 8–10 minutes. If the dough sticks while kneading, flour the work surface.

Kneading develops gluten, helping dough to rise

ANNE SAYS
"You can make and knead the dough in a heavy-duty electric mixer fitted with a dough hook."

4 Wash the large bowl and brush it with oil. Put the kneaded dough in the bowl and flip it so it is lightly oiled. Cover the bowl with a damp tea towel and let the dough rise in a warm place until doubled in bulk, 1–1 ½ hours.

3 SHAPE AND BAKE THE LOAVES

2 Cut the dough in half. Shape each piece of dough into a loose ball. Fold the sides over to the centre, turning and pinching to make a tight round ball. Put the balls, seam-side up, into the prepared bowls. Cover with dry tea towels, and let the loaves rise in a warm place until the bowls are just full, about 1 hour.

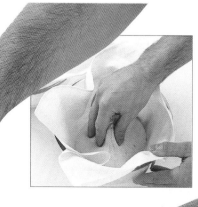

1 Line two 20 cm (8 inch) bowls with the pieces of cloth, and sprinkle generously with flour. Turn the dough onto the lightly floured work surface and knead just to knock out the air, 15–20 seconds. Cover the dough, and let rest, about 5 minutes.

3 Heat the oven to 200°C (400°F, Gas 6). Set the roasting tin to heat on the floor of the oven or on the lowest oven rack. Sprinkle the baking sheet with polenta. Turn the loaves, seam-side down, out of the bowls, onto the prepared baking sheets. With the scalpel, make 3 parallel slashes, 1.25 cm (1/2 inch) deep, in the top of each loaf, then make 3 more slashes to form a criss-cross pattern.

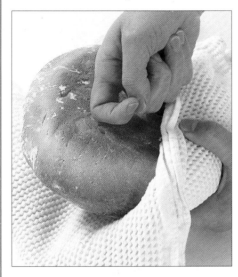

4 Put the loaves in the heated oven. At once drop the ice cubes into the hot roasting tin, then bake the loaves, 20 minutes. Lower the heat to 190°C (375°F, Gas 5), and continue baking until well browned, 20–25 minutes longer. Turn the loaves over and tap the bottoms with your knuckles. The bread should sound hollow and the sides should feel crisp when pressed. Let the loaves cool on the wire rack.

ANNE SAYS
"As the ice cubes hit the hot roasting tin, steam is formed, giving the loaves a crisp crust."

❚◉❘ TO SERVE
Serve with a hearty seafood stew, such as *cioppino,* another San Francisco favourite.

Slashes in dough make an attractive finish for these loaves

Crisp-crusted sourdough has a large, open crumb

V A R I A T I O N
SOURDOUGH ROLLS
Sourdough bread is equally delicious when shaped into individual rolls. Dusted with flour and slashed on top, they are ideal for picnic lunches.

1 Make the starter and the sponge; make and knead the dough, and let it rise as directed in the main recipe. Sprinkle 2 baking sheets with polenta.
2 Knock the air out of the dough, and let rest as directed. Cut the dough in half. With your hands, roll 1 piece of dough into a cylinder about 5 cm (2 inches) in diameter. With a chef's knife, cut the cylinder into 6 pieces. Repeat to shape and divide the remaining dough.
3 Lightly flour the work surface. Cup a piece of dough under the palm of your hand and roll the dough in a circular motion so that it forms a smooth ball. Repeat to shape the remaining dough. Set the rolls on the prepared baking sheets. Cover the rolls, and let rise in a warm place until doubled in bulk, about 30 minutes.
4 Heat the oven to 200°C (400°F, Gas 6), and heat the roasting tin as directed. Lightly sprinkle each roll with flour, then with a scalpel, make an "x" in the centre of each roll. Bake as directed, until the rolls are golden and sound hollow when tapped, 25–30 minutes. Makes 12 rolls.

MULTI-GRAIN BREAKFAST BREAD

🍽 MAKES 2 MEDIUM LOAVES   🥄 WORK TIME 45–50 MINUTES*   🍲 BAKING TIME 40–45 MINUTES

EQUIPMENT

pastry brush

chef's knife

bowls

tea towels

medium saucepan   wire rack

chopping board

2 baking sheets

wooden spoon

This hearty bread combines rolled oats, wheat bran, polenta, wholemeal and strong white flours, with sunflower seeds for added crunch. Buttermilk softens the texture of the bread, which is shaped to resemble a tobacco pouch.

GETTING AHEAD

This bread is best on the day of baking, but can be tightly wrapped and kept for 2–3 days, or it can be frozen.
plus 2 1/2–3 hours rising time

metric	SHOPPING LIST	imperial
75 g	shelled sunflower seeds	2 1/2 oz
425 ml	buttermilk	14 fl oz
12.5 ml	dried yeast, or 15 g (1/2 oz) fresh yeast	2 1/2 tsp
60 ml	lukewarm water	4 tbsp
45 g	quick-cooking rolled oats	1 1/2 oz
45 g	wheat bran	1 1/2 oz
75 g	polenta (fine yellow cornmeal), more for baking sheet	2 1/2 oz
45 g	soft brown sugar	1 1/2 oz
15 ml	salt	1 tbsp
250 g	strong wholemeal flour	8 oz
250 g	unbleached strong white flour, more if needed	8 oz
	butter for bowl	
1	egg white for glaze	1

INGREDIENTS

shelled sunflower seeds

unbleached strong white flour

polenta

wheat bran

dried yeast

soft brown sugar

buttermilk

rolled oats

butter

egg white

strong wholemeal flour

ANNE SAYS
"Finely crushed bran cereal flakes can be used in place of wheat bran."

ORDER OF WORK

1 **PREPARE THE SEEDS; MAKE THE DOUGH AND LET IT RISE**

2 **SHAPE AND BAKE THE LOAVES**

1 PREPARE THE SEEDS; MAKE THE DOUGH AND LET IT RISE

1 Heat the oven to 180°C (350°F, Gas 4). Spread the seeds on a baking sheet and toast in the heated oven until lightly browned, stirring occasionally, so they colour evenly, 5–7 minutes. Let cool, then coarsely chop.

2 Pour the buttermilk into the saucepan. Heat just to lukewarm. Dissolve the yeast in the water (see box, right).

! TAKE CARE !
High heat will curdle buttermilk.

Buttermilk is used to soften texture of dough

3 Put the sunflower seeds, rolled oats, wheat bran, polenta, brown sugar, and salt in a large bowl. Add the dissolved yeast and buttermilk and mix with your hand. Stir in the wholemeal flour with half of the strong white flour and mix well with your hand.

4 Add the remaining strong white flour, 60 g (2 oz) at a time, mixing well after each addition.

5 Keep adding strong white flour until the dough pulls away from the side of the bowl in a ball. It should be soft and slightly sticky.

HOW TO DISSOLVE YEAST

Yeast is a living organism and grows fastest in a warm, moist environment. In bread making, it acts by fermenting the natural sugars in flour into tiny bubbles of carbon dioxide, which cause the dough to rise. During baking, the bubbles expand to give bread its characteristic texture and flavour. Yeast is available dried or fresh. It is activated by being dissolved in a warm liquid, usually water.

1 In a small bowl, sprinkle or crumble the yeast over lukewarm liquid.

ANNE SAYS
"At low temperatures, the yeast works slowly; above 54°C (130°F), most yeast will die. The liquid should be just warm to the touch, 43°–46°C (110°–115°F)."

2 Set aside for 2 minutes. Stir gently with a teaspoon, then leave until the yeast is completely dissolved, 2–3 minutes.

6 Turn the dough onto a floured
work surface. Sprinkle the dough
and your hands with strong white flour,
and begin to knead by holding the
dough with one hand and pushing it
away from you with the other.
Continue to knead by peeling the
dough from the surface. Give the
dough a quarter turn, and knead
until it is very smooth,
elastic, and forms a
ball, 8–10 minutes.
If the dough
sticks while
kneading, flour
the work surface.

Push dough
firmly against
work surface

7 Wash the large bowl and brush
it with melted butter. Put the
kneaded dough in the bowl, and flip it
so the surface is lightly buttered. Cover
the bowl with a damp tea towel and
let the dough rise in a warm place
until doubled in bulk, 1½–2 hours.

2 SHAPE AND BAKE THE LOAVES

1 Sprinkle the baking sheets with
polenta. Turn the dough onto a
lightly floured work surface and knead
with your hand just to knock out the
air, 15–20 seconds. Cover the dough,
and let rest, about 5 minutes.

2 With the chef's knife, cut
the dough in half. Flour
your hands and pat 1 piece
of dough into a 38 x 10 cm
(15 x 4 inch) rectangle,
leaving the corners rounded.

4 Cover with a dry tea
towel, and let the
loaves rise in a warm
place until doubled in
bulk, about 1 hour.

Cloth covers
dough loosely,
leaving room for
dough to rise

3 Fold the rectangle crossways
in half, gently pressing the
halves together. Transfer the loaf to
1 of the prepared baking sheets and
repeat to shape the remaining dough.

Polenta on
baking sheet
keeps dough
from sticking

5 Heat the oven to 190°C (375°F, Gas 5). Make the glaze: beat the egg white just until frothy. Brush the loaves with the glaze.

6 Bake the loaves in the heated oven until well browned, 40–45 minutes. Turn the loaves over and tap the bottoms with your knuckles. The bread should sound hollow and the sides should feel crisp when pressed. Transfer the loaves to the wire rack and let cool completely.

Bottom of bread is nicely browned

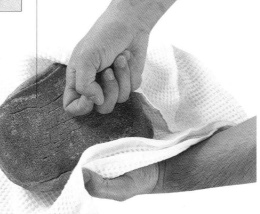

🍴 TO SERVE
Serve this hearty bread plain or toasted. It is delicious for breakfast with eggs and bacon.

Egg-white glaze gives bread a shiny finish

Assorted seeds and grains make this a tasty loaf

VARIATION

ORANGE JUICE BREAKFAST BREAD

Here, orange juice replaces the buttermilk, and the dough is snipped for a decorative "hedgehog" finish. Use freshly squeezed orange juice if you can.

1 Omit the sunflower seeds and buttermilk. Allow 425 ml (14 fl oz) orange juice to come to room temperature. Make the dough, using the orange juice in place of the buttermilk, but do not heat it. Knead the dough, and let rise as directed.
2 Sprinkle a baking sheet with polenta. Knock the air out of the dough and let rest as directed. Cut the dough in half. Flour your hands and pat 1 piece of dough into an oval about 25 cm (10 inches) long. Gently roll the dough back and forth on the work surface, exerting more pressure on the ends to taper them. Transfer the loaf to the prepared baking sheet. Repeat to shape the remaining dough. Cover the loaves, and let rise as directed.
3 Heat the oven to 190°C (375°F, Gas 5). Glaze the loaves as directed, then snip them deeply all over with kitchen scissors, lifting as you cut to make points of dough. Bake and let cool as directed.

FRENCH BAGUETTE

🍴 MAKES 3   🥣 WORK TIME 40–45 MINUTES*   ♨ BAKING TIME 25–30 MINUTES

EQUIPMENT

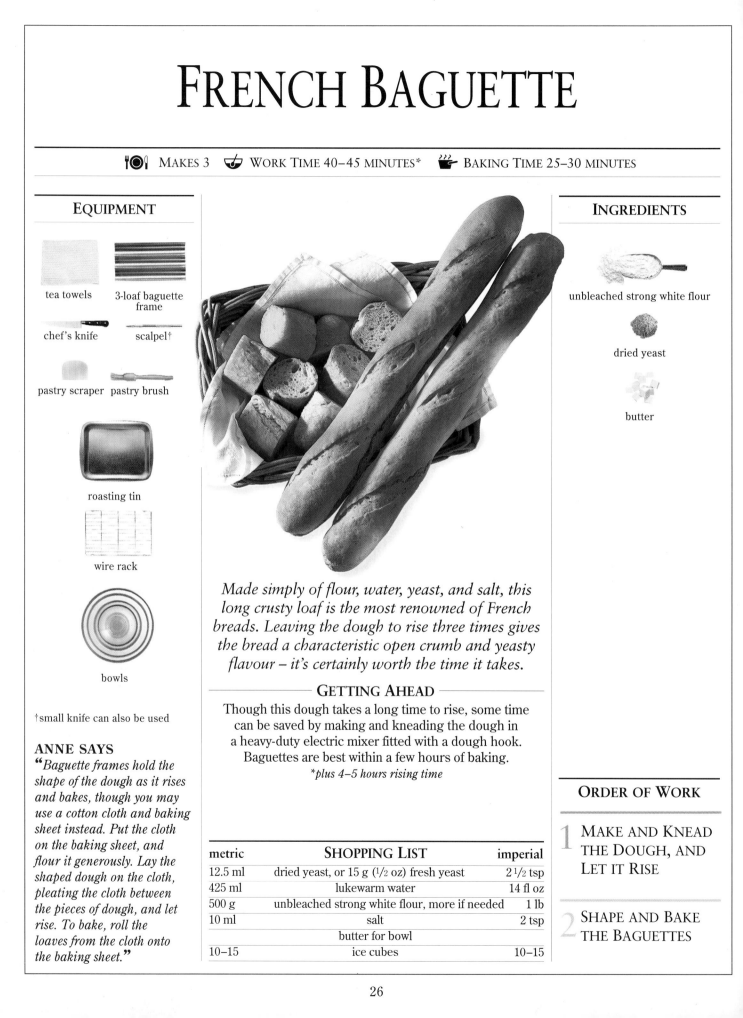

tea towels

3-loaf baguette frame

chef's knife

scalpel†

pastry scraper

pastry brush

roasting tin

wire rack

bowls

†small knife can also be used

ANNE SAYS
"Baguette frames hold the shape of the dough as it rises and bakes, though you may use a cotton cloth and baking sheet instead. Put the cloth on the baking sheet, and flour it generously. Lay the shaped dough on the cloth, pleating the cloth between the pieces of dough, and let rise. To bake, roll the loaves from the cloth onto the baking sheet."

INGREDIENTS

unbleached strong white flour

dried yeast

butter

Made simply of flour, water, yeast, and salt, this long crusty loaf is the most renowned of French breads. Leaving the dough to rise three times gives the bread a characteristic open crumb and yeasty flavour – it's certainly worth the time it takes.

GETTING AHEAD
Though this dough takes a long time to rise, some time can be saved by making and kneading the dough in a heavy-duty electric mixer fitted with a dough hook. Baguettes are best within a few hours of baking.
plus 4–5 hours rising time

metric	SHOPPING LIST	imperial
12.5 ml	dried yeast, or 15 g (1/2 oz) fresh yeast	2 1/2 tsp
425 ml	lukewarm water	14 fl oz
500 g	unbleached strong white flour, more if needed	1 lb
10 ml	salt	2 tsp
	butter for bowl	
10–15	ice cubes	10–15

ORDER OF WORK

1   MAKE AND KNEAD THE DOUGH, AND LET IT RISE

2   SHAPE AND BAKE THE BAGUETTES

1 MAKE AND KNEAD THE DOUGH, AND LET IT RISE

1 In a small bowl, sprinkle or crumble the yeast over 60 ml (4 tbsp) of the water. Let stand until dissolved, stirring once, about 5 minutes.

2 Put the flour onto a work surface with the salt. Make a large well in the centre and add the dissolved yeast and remaining water. With your fingertips, work the ingredients in the well until thoroughly mixed.

Work in any remaining flour while kneading

3 Gradually draw in the flour with the pastry scraper and work it into the liquid ingredients with your hand to form a smooth dough. It should be soft and slightly sticky.

Dough becomes less sticky and more elastic during kneading

4 Sprinkle the dough with flour, and begin to knead by holding the dough with one hand and pushing it away from you with the other.

5 Continue to knead by peeling the dough from the work surface. Give the dough a quarter turn, and knead until it is very smooth, elastic, and forms a ball, 5–7 minutes. If the dough sticks while kneading, flour the work surface sparingly.

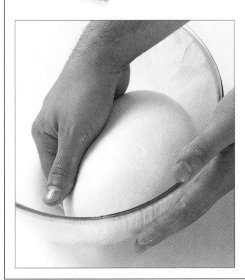

6 Brush a large bowl with melted butter. Put the kneaded dough in the bowl, and flip it so the surface is lightly buttered. Cover the bowl with a damp tea towel and let the dough rise in a warm place until tripled in bulk, 2–2 1/2 hours. Turn the dough onto a lightly floured work surface and knead with your hand just to knock out the air, 15–20 seconds.

7 Return the dough to the bowl, cover, and let rise in a warm place until doubled in bulk, 1–1 1/2 hours.

27

2 SHAPE AND BAKE THE BAGUETTES

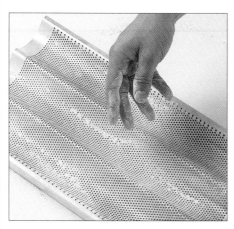

1 Sprinkle the baguette frame with flour. Turn the dough onto a lightly floured work surface and knead with your hand just to knock out the air, 15–20 seconds. Cover the dough, and let rest, about 5 minutes.

2 With the chef's knife, cut straight down through the dough, dividing it into 3 equal pieces.

Cut straight down; avoid dragging knife through dough

3 Cover 2 pieces of dough while shaping the other. Flour your hands and pat 1 piece of dough into an 18 x 10 cm (7 x 4 inch) rectangle.

ANNE SAYS
"*Pressing the dough into a rectangle breaks any remaining air pockets, improving its texture.*"

Apply even pressure while rolling cylinder

4 Starting with a long side, roll the rectangle into a cylinder, pinching and sealing it with your fingers as you go. With the palms of your hands, roll the cylinder, stretching it until it is a stick shape about 40 cm (16 inches) long.

ANNE SAYS
"*Pinch the cylinder firmly for a well-textured loaf; when rolling, move your hands from the centre to the ends to keep the loaf even in shape. Flour hands and the work surface as necessary—too much flour and the dough will slide, too little and it will stick*"

5 Put the shaped loaf into the prepared baguette frame. Repeat to shape the remaining dough.

Frame holds baguettes in shape while dough rises

6 Cover the frame with a dry tea towel, and let the dough rise in a warm place until doubled in bulk, about 1 hour.

7 Heat the oven to 220°C (425°F, Gas 7). Set the roasting tin to heat on the floor of the oven or on the lowest oven rack. With the scalpel, make 3 long, slightly diagonal slashes, 5 mm (¼ inch) deep, in each loaf.

Slash allows steam to escape while loaf bakes

8 Put the frame holding the loaves into the heated oven. At once drop the ice cubes into the hot roasting tin. Bake the loaves until well browned, 25–30 minutes. Turn them over and tap the bottoms with your knuckles. The bread should sound hollow and the sides should feel crisp when pressed. Let cool completely.

ANNE SAYS
"As the ice cubes hit the hot roasting tin, steam is formed, giving the loaves a crisp crust."

¶◉¶ TO SERVE
Baguette is traditionally served plain, but can be split, spread with butter, and layered with ham, pâté, or cheese.

Large, open crumb is characteristic of baguette

Crust is crisp golden brown

WHEAT EAR BAGUETTE
These baguettes are shaped to resemble ears of wheat. In France, this bread is called épi.

1 Make and knead the dough, and let it rise, first until tripled in bulk, then until doubled, as directed.
2 Press a dry tea towel into the curves of a baguette frame, pleating it between each depression. Sprinkle it generously with flour. Knock the air out of the dough as directed. Shape the loaves, rolling each to a length of 35 cm (14 inches). Put the loaves in the baguette frame. Let rise.
3 Sprinkle 2 baking sheets with flour. Lift the loaves on the cloth, keeping the pleats intact, onto 1 of the prepared baking sheets. Lift 1 pleat so 2 loaves roll onto the baking sheet. Place them 15 cm (6 inches) apart. Roll the third loaf onto the other baking sheet.
4 Heat the oven and a roasting tin as directed. Make a V-shaped cut about halfway through 1 of the loaves, 5–7 cm (2–3 inches) from the end. Pull the point to the left. Make a second cut 5–7 cm (2–3 inches) from the first, pulling the point to the right. Continue to shape the remaining dough. Bake and let cool as directed.

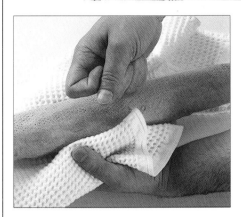

SEEDED RYE BREAD

🍽 MAKES 1 MEDIUM LOAF   🥣 WORK TIME 35–40 MINUTES*   🍲 BAKING TIME 50–55 MINUTES

EQUIPMENT

baking sheet

bowls

wire rack

tea towels

scalpel†

†small knife can also be used

ANNE SAYS
"You can make and knead the dough in a heavy-duty electric mixer fitted with a dough hook, or in a food processor."

Rye flour is darker than wheat flour, producing a crusty loaf that is full of flavour, accented here by caraway seeds. Because rye flour is low in gluten, I've mixed it with strong flour, which is slightly higher in gluten, to lighten the texture of the loaf.

GETTING AHEAD

Rye bread is best on the day of baking, but can be tightly wrapped and kept 1–2 days, or it can be frozen.

*plus 2¼–2¾ hours rising time

INGREDIENTS

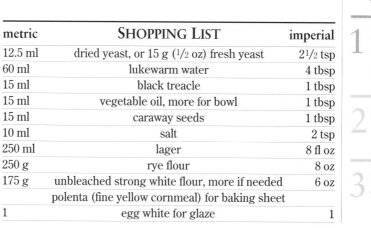

caraway seeds

rye flour

unbleached strong white flour

egg white

vegetable oil

lager

dried yeast

polenta

black treacle

ANNE SAYS
"Any kind of lager can be used, but I find Pils works particularly well with this rye dough."

ORDER OF WORK

1   MAKE AND KNEAD THE DOUGH, AND LET IT RISE

2   SHAPE THE LOAF

3   GLAZE AND BAKE THE LOAF

metric	SHOPPING LIST	imperial
12.5 ml	dried yeast, or 15 g (½ oz) fresh yeast	2½ tsp
60 ml	lukewarm water	4 tbsp
15 ml	black treacle	1 tbsp
15 ml	vegetable oil, more for bowl	1 tbsp
15 ml	caraway seeds	1 tbsp
10 ml	salt	2 tsp
250 ml	lager	8 fl oz
250 g	rye flour	8 oz
175 g	unbleached strong white flour, more if needed	6 oz
	polenta (fine yellow cornmeal) for baking sheet	
1	egg white for glaze	1

1 MAKE AND KNEAD THE DOUGH, AND LET IT RISE

1 In a small bowl, sprinkle the yeast over the water. Let stand until dissolved, stirring once, about 5 minutes.

2 Put the dissolved yeast, black treacle, oil, two-thirds of the caraway seeds, and the salt into a large bowl. Pour in the lager. Stir in the rye flour and mix well with your hand.

Lager adds characteristic yeasty flavour

Warmth from your hands helps activate yeast

3 Add the strong flour, 60 g (2 oz) at a time, mixing well after each addition.

4 Keep adding strong flour until the dough pulls away from the side of the bowl in a ball. It should be soft and slightly sticky.

5 Turn the dough onto a floured surface. Sprinkle the dough with flour, and begin to knead by holding the dough with one hand and pushing it away from you with the other.

! TAKE CARE !
Use white flour, not rye, for the work surface and your hands.

6 Continue to knead by peeling the dough from the surface. Give the dough a quarter turn, and knead until it is very smooth, elastic, and forms a ball, 8–10 minutes.

ANNE SAYS
"Kneading is more effective when you develop a regular, rhythmic action."

7 Wash the large bowl and brush it with oil. Put the kneaded dough in the bowl, and flip it so the surface is lightly oiled. Cover the bowl with a damp tea towel and let the dough rise in a warm place until doubled in bulk, 1½–2 hours.

2 SHAPE THE LOAF

1 Sprinkle the baking sheet with polenta. Turn the dough onto a lightly floured work surface and knead with your hand just to knock out the air, 15–20 seconds. Cover the dough, and let rest, about 5 minutes.

2 Flour your hands and pat the dough into an oval about 25 cm (10 inches) long.

Dough is quickly shaped into rough oval

3 Gently roll the dough back and forth on the work surface, exerting more pressure on the ends to taper them. Transfer the loaf to the prepared baking sheet.

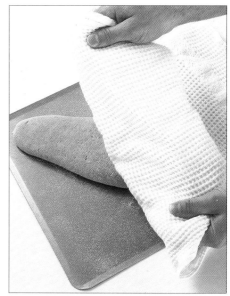

Centre of dough is thicker than ends

Each end of loaf is tapered

4 Cover the loaf with a dry tea towel, and let rise in a warm place until doubled in bulk, about 45 minutes.

3 GLAZE AND BAKE THE LOAF

2 Sprinkle the loaf with the remaining caraway seeds, and press them into the dough.

Caraway seeds stick easily to egg white

1 Heat the oven to 190°C (375°F, Gas 5). Beat the egg white until frothy. Brush the loaf with the glaze.

3 With the scalpel, make 3 diagonal slashes, about 5 mm (1/4 inch) deep, in the top of the loaf.

4 Bake the loaf in the heated oven until well browned, 50–55 minutes. Turn the loaf over and tap the bottom with your knuckles. The bread should sound hollow and the sides should feel crisp when pressed. Transfer the bread to the wire rack and let cool completely.

Tap centre of bread to check if done

Hold hot loaf with tea towel

¶◎¶ TO SERVE
Serve rye bread sliced. It is especially good with cheese, cooked meats, and cole slaw.

Bread is cut into thick slices for serving

Caraway seeds are classic garnish for rye bread

HORSESHOE RYE BREAD

The caraway seeds are omitted in this variation of rye bread. The dough is shaped into a horseshoe for a crusty loaf.

1 Omit the caraway seeds. Make and knead the dough, and let it rise as directed.

2 Sprinkle a baking sheet with polenta. Knock the air out of the dough, and let rest as directed. Flour your hands and pat the dough into a 25 x 20 cm (10 x 8 inch) rectangle. Starting with a long side, roll the rectangle into a cylinder, pinching and sealing it with your fingers as you go. With the palms of your hands, roll the cylinder until it is about 45 cm (18 inches) long. Transfer the cylinder, seam-side down, to the prepared baking sheet, then curve the ends around to form a horseshoe.

3 Cover the loaf, and let rise as directed. Heat the oven to 190°C (375°F, Gas 5). Make the glaze and brush the loaf with egg white as directed. With a scalpel, make a slash, 5 mm (1/4 inch) deep, along the top, following the curve of the loaf. Bake the loaf, and let cool as directed.

DINNER ROLLS

¶⊙¶ MAKES 16   ⤵ WORK TIME 45–55 MINUTES*   ♨ BAKING TIME 15–18 MINUTES

EQUIPMENT

wooden spoon

chef's knife

saucepan   pastry brush

bowls

2 baking sheets

tea towels

ANNE SAYS
"You can make and knead the dough in a heavy-duty electric mixer fitted with a dough hook."

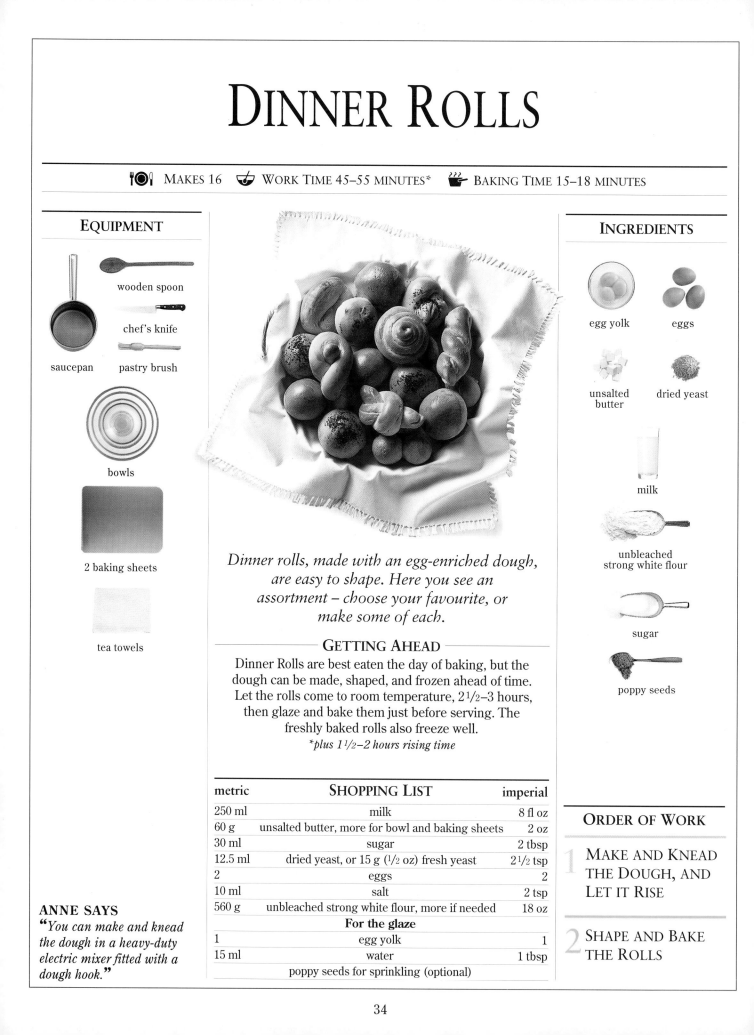

Dinner rolls, made with an egg-enriched dough, are easy to shape. Here you see an assortment – choose your favourite, or make some of each.

GETTING AHEAD

Dinner Rolls are best eaten the day of baking, but the dough can be made, shaped, and frozen ahead of time. Let the rolls come to room temperature, 2 1/2–3 hours, then glaze and bake them just before serving. The freshly baked rolls also freeze well.
plus 1 1/2–2 hours rising time

metric	SHOPPING LIST	imperial
250 ml	milk	8 fl oz
60 g	unsalted butter, more for bowl and baking sheets	2 oz
30 ml	sugar	2 tbsp
12.5 ml	dried yeast, or 15 g (1/2 oz) fresh yeast	2 1/2 tsp
2	eggs	2
10 ml	salt	2 tsp
560 g	unbleached strong white flour, more if needed	18 oz
	For the glaze	
1	egg yolk	1
15 ml	water	1 tbsp
	poppy seeds for sprinkling (optional)	

INGREDIENTS

egg yolk   eggs

unsalted butter   dried yeast

milk

unbleached strong white flour

sugar

poppy seeds

ORDER OF WORK

1 MAKE AND KNEAD THE DOUGH, AND LET IT RISE

2 SHAPE AND BAKE THE ROLLS

1 MAKE AND KNEAD THE DOUGH, AND LET IT RISE

1 Put the milk into the saucepan and bring just to a boil. Pour 60 ml (4 tbsp) of the milk into a small bowl and let cool to lukewarm. Meanwhile, cut the butter into pieces.

2 Add the butter and sugar to the remaining milk in the pan, stirring occasionally, until the butter is melted. Let cool to lukewarm.

Liquid ingredients are combined first

3 Sprinkle the yeast over the 60 ml (4 tbsp) milk and let stand, stirring once, until dissolved, about 5 minutes.

! TAKE CARE !
Milk that is too hot may kill the yeast.

4 In a large bowl, beat the eggs just until mixed. Add the cooled sweetened milk, salt, and dissolved yeast.

Mix dough vigorously with hand

Kneading develops gluten, helping dough to rise

5 Stir in half of the flour and mix well with your hand. Add the remaining flour, 60 g (2 oz) at a time, mixing well after each addition. Keep adding flour until the dough pulls away from the side of the bowl in a ball. It should be soft and slightly sticky.

6 Turn the dough onto a floured work surface. Sprinkle the dough and your hands with flour, and begin to knead by holding the dough with one hand and pushing it away from you with the other.

Dough is smooth
from kneading

Light coating of
butter will keep
dough moist

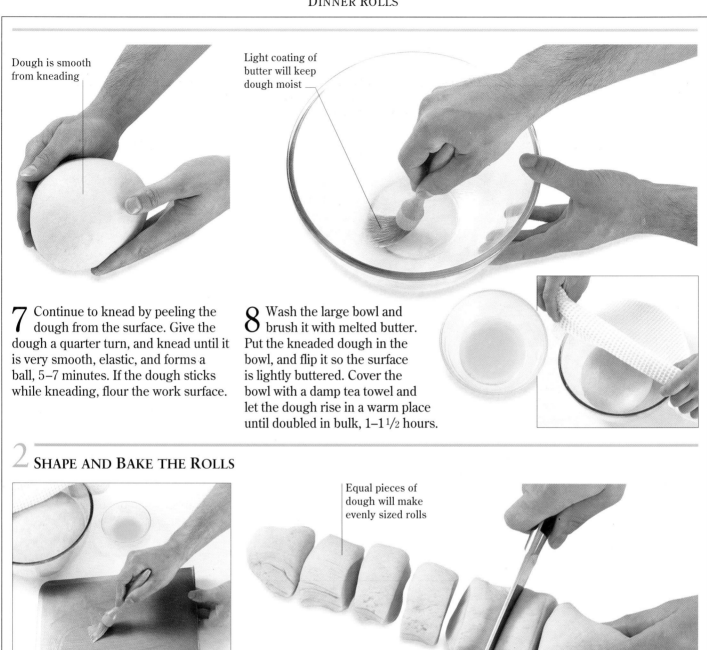

7 Continue to knead by peeling the dough from the surface. Give the dough a quarter turn, and knead until it is very smooth, elastic, and forms a ball, 5–7 minutes. If the dough sticks while kneading, flour the work surface.

8 Wash the large bowl and brush it with melted butter. Put the kneaded dough in the bowl, and flip it so the surface is lightly buttered. Cover the bowl with a damp tea towel and let the dough rise in a warm place until doubled in bulk, 1–1 1/2 hours.

2 SHAPE AND BAKE THE ROLLS

Equal pieces of
dough will make
evenly sized rolls

1 Brush the baking sheets with melted butter. Turn the dough onto a lightly floured work surface and knead with your hand just to knock out the air, 15–20 seconds. Cover the dough, and let rest, about 5 minutes.

2 Cut the dough in half. With your hands, roll 1 piece of the dough into a cylinder about 5 cm (2 inches) in diameter. Cut the cylinder into 8 equal pieces. Repeat to divide the remaining dough.

Roll dough firmly for
tight, round balls

3 To shape round rolls, cup a piece of dough under the palm of your hand, and roll the dough in a circular motion so it forms a smooth ball. For other shapes, see box, page 37.

4 Arrange 8 rolls on each baking sheet. Cover with a dry tea towel, and let rise in a warm place until doubled in bulk, about 30 minutes.

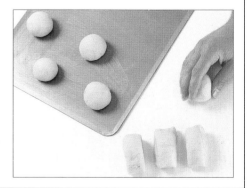

DECORATIVE ROLLS

*Rolls are easy to shape. When shaping the dough, use only a small amount of flour on your hands
and on the work surface: too much flour will change the consistency
of the dough, making it dry and stiff.*

PARKER HOUSE

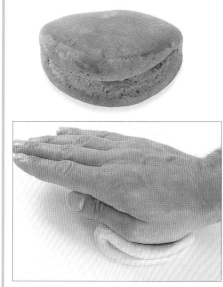

1 Make a round roll, then pat it flat, until 1 cm (³/8 inch) thick.

2 Brush the round with melted butter, fold, and press.

BOW KNOT

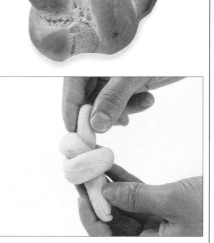

1 Roll a piece of dough into a long rope.

2 Tie a single knot, pulling through the ends of the rope.

BAKER'S KNOT

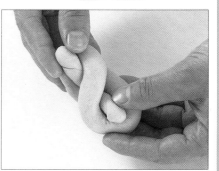

1 Roll a piece of dough into a long rope.

2 Shape into a figure of eight, and tuck the ends through the holes.

TWIST

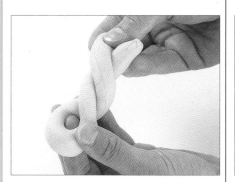

1 Roll a piece of dough into a long rope, fold it in half, and twist.

2 Arrange the twist on a baking sheet and press down the ends.

SNAIL

1 Roll a piece of dough into a long rope.

2 Wind the rope around in a spiral, tucking the end underneath.

CLOVER LEAF

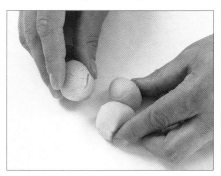

1 Divide a piece of dough into thirds and shape into small balls.

2 Push the balls close together so they are touching.

Brush tops and sides of dough with glaze

5 Heat the oven to 220°C (425°F, Gas 7). Make the glaze: beat the egg yolk with the water until frothy.

6 Brush the rolls with glaze, sprinkle with poppy seeds, if you like, then bake them in the heated oven until golden brown, 15–18 minutes.

7 Turn over the rolls and tap the bottoms with your knuckles. They should sound hollow when tapped.

Tap centre of roll

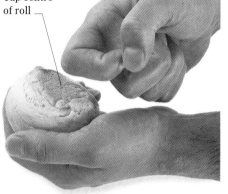

Egg glaze bakes to a golden brown

🍽 **TO SERVE**
Serve the rolls warm from the oven, piled in a basket. Spread them with butter, if you like.

Poppy seeds make an attractive decoration for rolls

38

VARIATION

CHALLAH

This traditional Jewish bread is baked for holidays and the Sabbath. It is usually, but not always, plaited. Challah, *meaning offering in Hebrew, dates from the third century BC, when Jews baked the loaves to bring to the temple.*

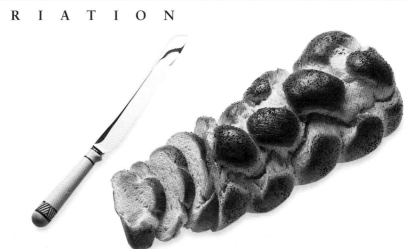

1 Make the dough, using 250 ml (8 fl oz) lukewarm water instead of milk, 60 ml (4 tbsp) vegetable oil instead of butter, and an additional 30 ml (2 tbsp) sugar; knead, and let rise as directed. Brush a baking sheet with oil. Knock the air out of the dough, and let rest.

2 Cut the dough into 4 equal pieces. Flour the work surface. Roll each piece of dough with the palms of your hands, stretching it to form a 63 cm (25 inch) strand. Make a plaited loaf (see box, below). Transfer the loaf to the prepared baking sheet.

3 Cover, and let rise until doubled in bulk, about 45 minutes. Heat the oven to 190°C (375°F, Gas 5). Glaze as directed, sprinkle with 5 ml (1 tsp) poppy seeds, and bake until golden and the bread sounds hollow when the bottom is tapped, 35–40 minutes.

HOW TO MAKE A PLAITED LOAF

Plaited loaves are usually made using 3 or 4 strands of dough. More decorative loaves are made with as many as 8 or 12 strands.

1 Line the strands up next to each other. Starting from your left, lift the first strand to cross over the second.

2 Lift the third strand to cross over the fourth. Now lift the fourth strand and lay it between the first and second strands.

Plait strands as evenly as possible

3 Continue plaiting: starting again from your left, lift the first strand to cross over the second. Lift the third strand to cross over the fourth. Now lift the fourth strand and lay it between the first and second strands.

4 Finish plaiting the strands, pinching the ends together and tucking them under the plaited loaf.

KUGELHOPF WITH WALNUTS, BACON, AND HERBS

🍴 MAKES 1 LARGE LOAF   🥣 WORK TIME 45–50 MINUTES*   🍲 BAKING TIME 45–50 MINUTES

EQUIPMENT

chef's knife

pastry brush

1 litre (1²/³ pint)
kugelhopf mould†

wire rack

saucepan

sieve

tea towels

paper towels

frying pan

pastry
scraper

chopping board

bowls

slotted spoon

†1 litre (1²/³ pint) ring mould can
also be used

This yeast bread from Alsace, the most easterly province of France, is traditionally baked in a decorative ring mould, which gives the loaf its characteristic shape. Slice the bread to reveal savoury walnuts, bacon, and fresh herbs.

GETTING AHEAD

Kugelhopf is best on the day of baking, but can be tightly wrapped and kept 2–3 days, or it can be frozen.
plus 1¹/₂–2¹/₄ hours rising time

INGREDIENTS

bacon

walnut halves

fresh thyme

fresh sage

unsalted butter

dried yeast

eggs

milk

unbleached strong white flour

sugar

metric	SHOPPING LIST	imperial
250 ml	milk	8 fl oz
150 g	unsalted butter, more for kugelhopf mould	5 oz
15 ml	sugar	1 tbsp
15 ml	dried yeast, or 20 g (²/³ oz) fresh yeast	1 tbsp
3	eggs	3
500 g	unbleached strong white flour	1 lb
5 ml	salt	1 tsp
3–5	sprigs of fresh sage	3–5
3–5	sprigs of fresh thyme	3–5
60 g	walnut halves	2 oz
125 g	thick-cut bacon rashers	4 oz

ORDER OF WORK

1 MAKE AND KNEAD THE DOUGH, AND LET IT RISE

2 PREPARE OTHER INGREDIENTS

3 FINISH AND BAKE THE KUGELHOPF

MAKE AND KNEAD THE DOUGH, AND LET IT RISE

1 Bring the milk just to a boil, pour 60 ml (4 tbsp) into a bowl, and let cool to lukewarm. Cut the butter into pieces. Add the butter and sugar to the milk in the pan, and stir until melted.

2 Sprinkle the yeast over the 60 ml (4 tbsp) milk and let stand until dissolved, stirring once, 5 minutes.

! TAKE CARE !
Milk that is too hot may kill the yeast.

3 Beat the eggs just until mixed. Sift the flour and salt into a large bowl. Make a well in the centre and add the dissolved yeast, eggs, and the cooled sweetened milk.

4 With your fingertips, work the ingredients in the well until thoroughly mixed.

5 Gradually draw in the flour and work it into the other ingredients with your hand to form a smooth dough.

6 Beat the dough: cupping your hand like a spoon, lift the dough, then let it fall back into the bowl with a slap. Continue beating the dough until it is very elastic, 5–7 minutes. You may tilt the bowl slightly to make beating easier.

! TAKE CARE !
Do not be tempted to add more flour to this dough when kneading; it should be very sticky.

Dough will become more elastic during kneading

7 Cover the bowl with a damp tea towel and let the dough rise in a warm place until doubled in bulk, 1–1½ hours. Meanwhile, prepare the other ingredients.

ANNE SAYS
"The flavour of the dough develops as the dough rises."

HOW TO CHOP HERBS

Sage, thyme, parsley, rosemary, and tarragon are herbs that are usually chopped before being added to other ingredients. Do not chop delicate herbs like basil too finely because they bruise easily.

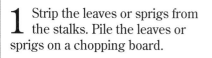

1 Strip the leaves or sprigs from the stalks. Pile the leaves or sprigs on a chopping board.

2 With a chef's knife, cut the herbs into small pieces. Holding the tip of the blade against the board and rocking the knife back and forth, chop until the herbs are coarse or fine.

ANNE SAYS
"Make sure your knife is very sharp, otherwise you will bruise the herbs rather than cut them."

2 PREPARE OTHER INGREDIENTS

1 Brush the kugelhopf mould with melted butter. Freeze the mould until the butter is hard, about 10 minutes, then butter it again.

2 Chop the herbs (see box, left). Set 5 walnut halves aside for decoration. With the chef's knife, coarsely chop the remaining walnuts.

3 Stack the bacon rashers on the chopping board and cut them crossways into strips. Cook the bacon, stirring occasionally, until lightly browned, 3–4 minutes. With the slotted spoon, transfer the bacon to paper towels and let drain.

Paper towel absorbs excess bacon fat

3 FINISH AND BAKE THE KUGELHOPF

1 Beat the dough lightly with your hand just to knock out the air, 15–20 seconds. Add the herbs, chopped walnuts, and bacon and beat with your hand until well combined.

2 Arrange the reserved walnut halves in a circle in the bottom of the prepared mould, placing them rounded-side down in the depressions.

3 Using the pastry scraper, drop the dough into the mould, filling it evenly. Cover the mould with a dry tea towel, and let the dough rise in a warm place until just above the top of the mould, 30–40 minutes.

Drop dough gently to keep walnut halves in place

Walnut halves are attractive decoration for buttery kugelhopf

4 Heat the oven to 190°C (375°F, Gas 5). Bake the kugelhopf in the heated oven until puffed and very brown, and the bread starts to shrink from the side of the mould, 45–50 minutes. Let it cool slightly. Unmould the bread onto the wire rack and let cool completely.

🍴 TO SERVE

Serve the kugelhopf sliced, as an accompaniment to soups or simple salads.

Bacon is savoury and tender

VARIATION

KUGELHOPF WITH RAISINS AND ALMONDS

Dark raisins and chopped almonds are baked in this classic kugelhopf – an Alsatian favourite. A dusting of icing sugar hints at the sweet filling.

1 Omit the herbs, walnuts, and bacon. Bring the milk just to a boil. Let 60 ml (4 tbsp) of the milk cool to lukewarm. Melt the butter as directed, adding 60 g (2 oz) granulated sugar. Dissolve the yeast; make and knead the dough, and let it rise as directed.

2 Prepare the kugelhopf mould as directed. Put 90 g (3 oz) raisins into a small bowl and pour over hot water to cover. Let the raisins soak until plump, 10–15 minutes, then drain thoroughly. Set 7 whole blanched almonds aside for decoration. Coarsely chop 60 g (2 oz) whole blanched almonds. Arrange the reserved almonds, alternating with 7 soaked raisins, in the bottom of the prepared mould.

3 Mix the remaining raisins and chopped almonds into the kugelhopf dough in place of the herbs, walnuts, and bacon. Finish, bake, unmould, and let cool as directed. Just before serving, sift 15 ml (1 tbsp) icing sugar over the kugelhopf.

ONION AND WALNUT CROWN

🍽 MAKES 1 LARGE LOAF   🥣 WORK TIME 40–45 MINUTES*   ☕ BAKING TIME 45–50 MINUTES

EQUIPMENT

bowls

kitchen scissors

pastry brush

chef's knife

pastry scraper

saucepan

wire rack

frying pan

tea towels

baking sheet

chopping board

wooden spoon

ANNE SAYS
"*You can make and knead the dough in a heavy-duty electric mixer fitted with a dough hook.*"

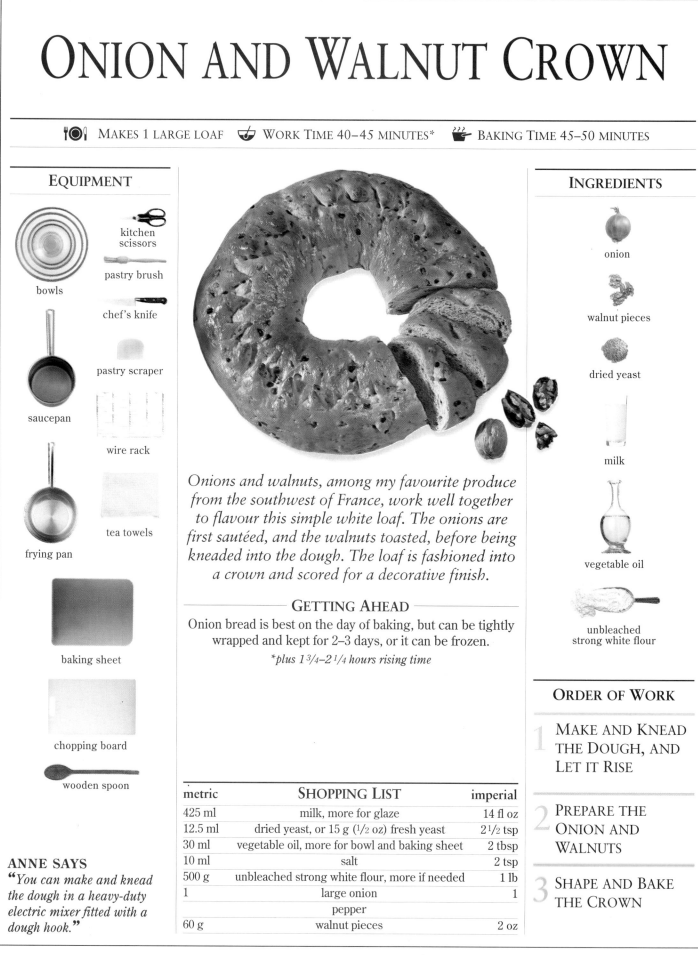

Onions and walnuts, among my favourite produce from the southwest of France, work well together to flavour this simple white loaf. The onions are first sautéed, and the walnuts toasted, before being kneaded into the dough. The loaf is fashioned into a crown and scored for a decorative finish.

GETTING AHEAD
Onion bread is best on the day of baking, but can be tightly wrapped and kept for 2–3 days, or it can be frozen.
*plus 1 3/4–2 1/4 hours rising time

INGREDIENTS

onion

walnut pieces

dried yeast

milk

vegetable oil

unbleached strong white flour

ORDER OF WORK

1 MAKE AND KNEAD THE DOUGH, AND LET IT RISE

2 PREPARE THE ONION AND WALNUTS

3 SHAPE AND BAKE THE CROWN

metric	SHOPPING LIST	imperial
425 ml	milk, more for glaze	14 fl oz
12.5 ml	dried yeast, or 15 g (1/2 oz) fresh yeast	2 1/2 tsp
30 ml	vegetable oil, more for bowl and baking sheet	2 tbsp
10 ml	salt	2 tsp
500 g	unbleached strong white flour, more if needed	1 lb
1	large onion	1
	pepper	
60 g	walnut pieces	2 oz

1 MAKE AND KNEAD THE DOUGH, AND LET IT RISE

1 Bring the milk just to a boil. Pour 60 ml (4 tbsp) of the milk into a small bowl and let cool to lukewarm.

2 Sprinkle or crumble the yeast over the 60 ml (4 tbsp) milk, and let stand, stirring once, until dissolved, about 5 minutes.

! TAKE CARE !
Milk that is too hot may kill the yeast.

Beat vigorously with hand for even mixing

3 Put the dissolved yeast, remaining milk, half of the oil, and the salt into a large bowl. Stir in half of the flour and mix well with your hand.

4 Add the remaining flour, 60 g (2 oz) at a time, mixing well after each addition. Keep adding flour until the dough pulls away from the side of the bowl in a ball. It should be soft and slightly sticky.

ANNE SAYS
"If flour remains, work it in while kneading the dough."

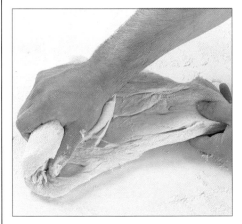

Damp tea towel helps prevent dough from drying out

5 Turn the dough onto a floured work surface. Sprinkle the dough and your hands with flour, and begin to knead by holding the dough with one hand and pushing it away from you with the other.

6 Continue to knead by peeling the dough from the surface. Give the dough a quarter turn, and knead until it is very smooth, elastic, and forms a ball, 5–7 minutes. If the dough sticks while kneading, flour the work surface.

7 Wash the large bowl and brush it with melted butter. Flip the dough in the bowl so it is lightly buttered. Cover with a damp tea towel and let rise in a warm place until doubled in bulk, 1–1½ hours.

2 PREPARE THE ONION AND WALNUTS

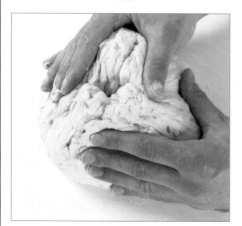

Use knuckles to guide knife

1 Heat the oven to 180°C (350°F, Gas 4). Peel the onion, and cut it lengthways in half. Set each half cut-side down and slice horizontally, then vertically towards the root, leaving the slices attached. Cut across into dice.

2 Heat the remaining oil in the frying pan. Add the chopped onion with salt and pepper and cook, stirring often, until soft and lightly brown, 5–7 minutes. Taste for seasoning and set aside to cool.

3 Spread the walnut pieces on the baking sheet and toast in the heated oven, stirring occasionally, until lightly browned, 8–10 minutes. Let the nuts cool, then coarsely chop them with the chef's knife.

3 SHAPE AND BAKE THE CROWN

Dough stiffens as air is knocked out

1 Brush the baking sheet with oil. Turn the dough onto a lightly floured work surface and knead with your hand just to knock out the air, 15–20 seconds. Cover the dough, and let rest, about 5 minutes.

2 Knead the onion and walnuts into the dough until evenly blended, 2–3 minutes. Cover the dough, and let rest, about 5 minutes longer.

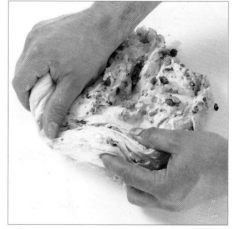

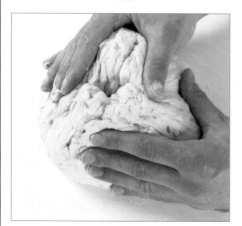

Use fingers to shape and stretch centre of ring

3 Shape the dough into a loose ball. Fold the sides over to the centre, turning and pinching to make a tight round ball. Flip the ball, seam-side down, onto the work surface.

4 Make a hole in the centre of the ball with two of your fingers. With your fingers, enlarge the hole, turning to make an even ring. Gradually enlarge the ring to a diameter of 25–30 cm (10–12 inches).

5 Lift the ring onto the prepared baking sheet. Cover the loaf with a dry tea towel, and let rise in a warm place until doubled in bulk, about 45 minutes.

6 Heat the oven to 200°C (400°F, Gas 6). Brush the ring with milk. With the kitchen scissors, snip around the top of the ring in a zig-zag design.

Cut about 5 mm (¼ inch) into dough

7 Bake the loaf in the heated oven until it is well browned, 45–50 minutes. Turn the loaf over and tap the bottom with your knuckles. The bread should sound hollow and the sides should feel crisp when pressed. Transfer the bread to the wire rack and let cool completely.

¶©¶ TO SERVE
Serve this bread plain or buttered, or as part of a ploughman's lunch of salad, cheese, chutney, and pickles.

Toasted walnuts, together with sautéed onions, add rich flavour to this simple white bread

VARIATION

GREEN AND BLACK OLIVE BREAD

Oil-cured green and black olives give this loaf a pungent, earthy flavour.

1 Omit the milk, vegetable oil, onion, pepper, and walnuts. Make the dough, using 375 ml (12 fl oz) lukewarm water in place of the milk and 15 ml (1 tbsp) olive oil instead of the vegetable oil. Knead the dough, and let rise as directed.
2 Meanwhile, stone and coarsely chop 100 g (3¼ oz) oil-cured green olives and 100 g (3¼ oz) oil-cured black olives. Brush a baking sheet with oil.
3 Knock the air out of the dough and let rest as directed. Knead the chopped olives into the dough as for the onion and walnuts, and let rest as directed. Flour your hands and pat the dough into an oval about 25 cm (10 inches) long. Gently roll the dough back and forth on the work surface. Transfer the dough to the prepared baking sheet. Cover the loaf and let rise as directed.
4 Heat the oven to 200°C (400°F, Gas 6). Sprinkle the loaf with flour. With a chef's knife, make a slash down the centre of the loaf, cutting all the way through the dough to the baking sheet. Bake the loaf and let cool as directed.

SMALL BRIOCHES

🍽️ MAKES 10   🥣 WORK TIME 45–50 MINUTES*   ☕ BAKING TIME 15–20 MINUTES

EQUIPMENT

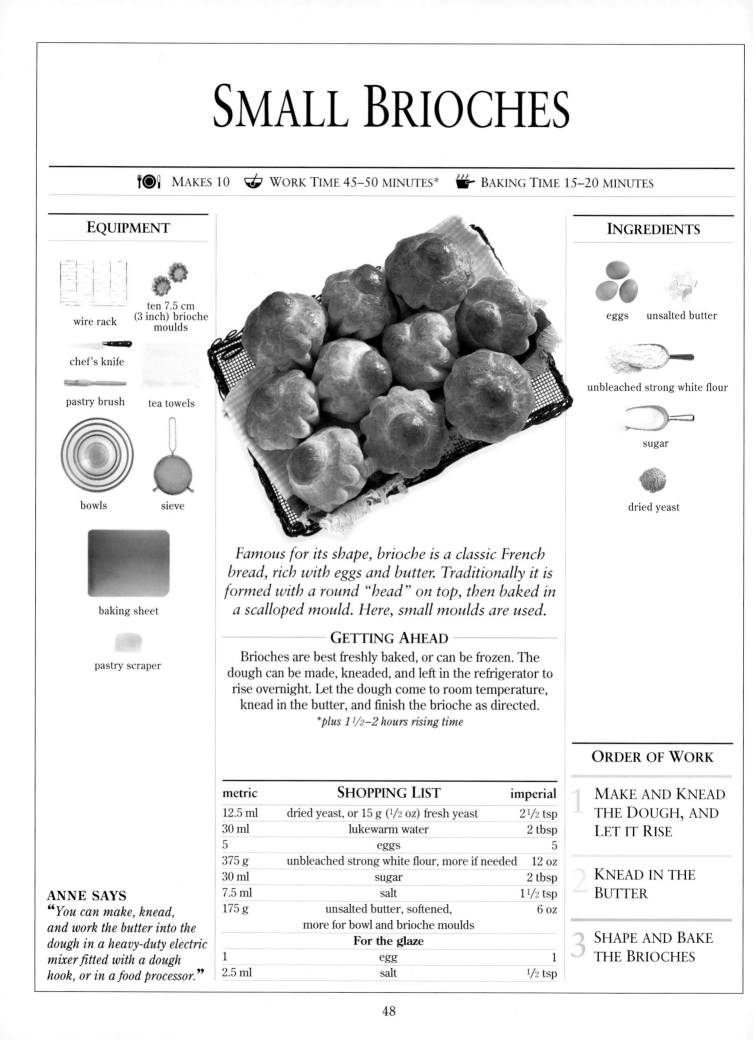

wire rack

ten 7.5 cm (3 inch) brioche moulds

chef's knife

pastry brush

tea towels

bowls

sieve

baking sheet

pastry scraper

ANNE SAYS
"You can make, knead, and work the butter into the dough in a heavy-duty electric mixer fitted with a dough hook, or in a food processor."

INGREDIENTS

eggs   unsalted butter

unbleached strong white flour

sugar

dried yeast

Famous for its shape, brioche is a classic French bread, rich with eggs and butter. Traditionally it is formed with a round "head" on top, then baked in a scalloped mould. Here, small moulds are used.

GETTING AHEAD
Brioches are best freshly baked, or can be frozen. The dough can be made, kneaded, and left in the refrigerator to rise overnight. Let the dough come to room temperature, knead in the butter, and finish the brioche as directed.
*plus 1 1/2–2 hours rising time

metric	SHOPPING LIST	imperial
12.5 ml	dried yeast, or 15 g (1/2 oz) fresh yeast	2 1/2 tsp
30 ml	lukewarm water	2 tbsp
5	eggs	5
375 g	unbleached strong white flour, more if needed	12 oz
30 ml	sugar	2 tbsp
7.5 ml	salt	1 1/2 tsp
175 g	unsalted butter, softened, more for bowl and brioche moulds	6 oz
For the glaze		
1	egg	1
2.5 ml	salt	1/2 tsp

ORDER OF WORK

1 MAKE AND KNEAD THE DOUGH, AND LET IT RISE

2 KNEAD IN THE BUTTER

3 SHAPE AND BAKE THE BRIOCHES

1 MAKE AND KNEAD THE DOUGH, AND LET IT RISE

1 In a small bowl, sprinkle or crumble the yeast over the water. Let stand until dissolved, stirring once, about 5 minutes.

2 In a small bowl, beat the eggs with a fork just until mixed.

3 Sift the flour onto the work surface with the sugar and salt. Make a large well in the centre and add the eggs and dissolved yeast. With your fingertips, work the ingredients in the well until thoroughly mixed.

Large well is needed to hold liquid ingredients

Beaten eggs add characteristic richness to brioche dough

4 Gradually draw in the flour with the pastry scraper and work it into the other ingredients with your hand to form a smooth dough. It should be soft and sticky.

5 Sprinkle the dough with flour and knead, lifting the dough up and throwing it down until it is very elastic and resembles chamois leather, 8–10 minutes. Work in more flour as necessary, so that at the end of kneading the dough is slightly sticky but peels easily from the work surface. It will become less sticky and more elastic while kneading, so add flour sparingly.

Damp tea towel keeps dough moist while it rises

Dough is lightly coated with melted butter

6 Brush a large bowl with melted butter. Put the kneaded dough into the bowl, and flip it, rolling it against the side of the bowl, so the surface is lightly buttered.

7 Cover the bowl with a damp tea towel and let the dough rise in a warm place until doubled in bulk, 1–1 1/2 hours. Alternatively, put the covered bowl of dough in the refrigerator and leave it up to 8 hours or overnight. It will rise slowly during that time.

2 KNEAD IN THE BUTTER

1 Brush the brioche moulds with melted butter. Set the moulds on the baking sheet.

Pastry brush reaches every part of mould

2 Turn the dough onto a lightly floured work surface and knead with your hand just to knock out the air, 15–20 seconds. Cover the dough, and let rest, about 5 minutes.

Double coating of melted butter prevents brioche sticking to mould

Squeeze dough to incorporate softened butter

3 Knead in the softened butter, pinching and squeezing the dough with both hands. Knead the dough on the floured work surface until smooth again, 3–5 minutes. Cover the dough, and let rest, 5 minutes more.

3 SHAPE AND BAKE THE BRIOCHES

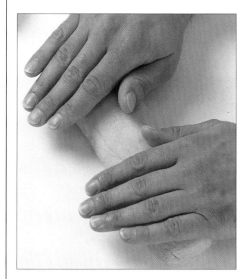

1 Cut the dough in half. Roll 1 piece of dough into a cylinder about 5 cm (2 inches) in diameter. Cut the cylinder into 5 pieces. Repeat to shape and divide the remaining dough.

Dough is fairly stiff and will hold its shape

2 Lightly flour the work surface. Cup each piece of dough under the palm of your hand and roll the dough in a circular motion so that it forms a smooth ball.

3 Pinch about one-quarter of each ball between your thumb and forefinger, almost dividing it from the remaining dough, to form the head.

4 Holding the head, lower each ball into a mould, twisting and pressing the head onto the base of the brioche.

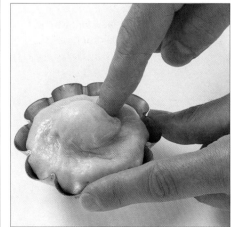

Cover loosely with tea towel so brioches have room to rise

5 With your forefinger, press down 2–3 times around the head to seal it to the base of the brioche.

6 Cover the moulds with a dry tea towel, and let the dough rise in a warm place until the moulds are full and the dough is puffed, about 30 minutes.

8 Unmould 1 of the brioches, turn it over and tap the bottom with your knuckles. It should sound hollow. Let them cool slightly, then unmould. Transfer to the wire rack and let cool completely.

Hold hot brioche with tea towel

Side and bottom of brioche are golden brown

7 Heat the oven to 220°C (425°F, Gas 7). Lightly beat the egg with the salt. Brush the brioches with egg glaze. Bake the brioches in the heated oven until puffed and brown, 15–20 minutes.

ANNE SAYS
"Good-quality butter makes the best brioche. Normandy and the Charentes, where the best French butter comes from, pride themselves on their brioche."

⦅◎⦆ TO SERVE
Brioches make a special breakfast or afternoon tea. Serve them plain, or with jam to spread on each bite.

Brioche is shaped with characteristic head on top

Egg glaze
bakes to a rich golden brown

RICH BRIOCHE

Here, brioche dough is shaped into large round loaves – its classic guise. More butter is kneaded in to make this variation quite rich. Serve it sliced, toasted and spread with jam.

1 Make and knead the dough, and let it rise as directed in the main recipe.

2 Brush two 17.5 cm (7 inch) brioche moulds with melted butter. Knock the air out of the dough, and let it rest as directed. Work 250 g (8 oz) plus 15 g (1/2 oz) softened unsalted butter into the dough until smooth.

3 Cut the dough in half. Pinch off one-third of each piece for the heads of the brioches. Shape all 4 pieces of dough into tight round balls. Put the large balls, seam-side down, into the prepared brioche moulds, making a depression in the centre of each ball. Set the small balls on top, pressing them to the bases as directed. Cover the moulds with a dry tea towel and let the dough rise in a warm place until the moulds are full, about 45 minutes.

4 Heat the oven to 200°C (400°F, Gas 6). Make the egg glaze and glaze the brioches as directed. Bake the loaves until puffed and brown, 25–30 minutes. Unmould the loaves, turn them over, and tap the bottoms with your knuckles. They should sound hollow when tapped. Let cool as directed. Makes 2 loaves.

CHEESE BRIOCHE

Brie adds ripe flavour to brioche when kneaded into the dough in place of some of the butter. Baked in a loaf tin, this rich bread is excellent sliced and eaten plain or toasted.

1 Make and knead the dough, and let it rise as directed in the main recipe. Brush a 23 x 13 x 7.5 cm (9 x 5 x 3 inch) loaf tin with melted butter. Cut the rind from 150 g (5 oz) Brie, cut the cheese into small chunks, and let it come to room temperature. Knock the air out of the dough, and let rest as directed. Work the cheese and 60 g (2 oz) softened unsalted butter into the dough until smooth.

2 Cut the dough in half. Roll each piece into a cylinder and cut each cylinder into 4 pieces. Roll each piece of dough into a ball as directed but do not form the head. Put the balls of dough into the prepared loaf tin, arranging them on a slight diagonal. Cover the tin as directed, and let the dough rise in a warm place until the tin is three-quarters full, about 45 minutes.

3 Heat the oven to 200°C (400°F, Gas 6). Glaze the loaf as directed. Bake the loaf until well browned and the brioche sounds hollow when the bottom is tapped, 30–35 minutes. Transfer to a wire rack and let cool completely. Makes 1 loaf.

POTATO-CHIVE MONKEY BREAD

¶◎⌇ MAKES 1 LARGE LOAF   **⊌ WORK TIME 50–55 MINUTES***   **♨ BAKING TIME 40–45 MINUTES**

EQUIPMENT

1.75 litre (3 pint) ring mould

potato masher

chef's knife

pastry brush

vegetable peeler

pastry scraper

bowls

wire rack

tea towels

small saucepan with lid

sieve

shallow dish

chopping board

ANNE SAYS
"You can make and knead the dough in a heavy-duty electric mixer with a dough hook, or in a food processor. Instead of a ring mould, you can use a 25 cm (10 inch) round cake tin, with a 250 ml (8 fl oz) ramekin upside-down in the centre."

Bread made with mashed potato has a soft crust and moist centre, and is an American favourite. In this recipe, fresh chives are kneaded into the dough, which is shaped into balls, coated in butter, and baked in a ring mould. The result is "monkey" bread, served by simply pulling it apart with your fingers.

GETTING AHEAD
Potato bread is delicious warm from the oven, but can be tightly wrapped and kept 2–3 days, or it can be frozen. The dough can be made, kneaded, and left to rise in the refrigerator overnight. Shape the dough, let it come to room temperature, then bake as directed.

*plus 1 1/2–2 1/4 hours rising time

metric	SHOPPING LIST	imperial
250 g	potatoes	8 oz
12.5 ml	dried yeast, or 15 g (1/2 oz) fresh yeast	2 1/2 tsp
60 ml	lukewarm water	4 tbsp
125 g	unsalted butter, more for bowl and ring mould	4 oz
1	large bunch of chives	1
30 ml	sugar	2 tbsp
10 ml	salt	2 tsp
425 g	unbleached strong white flour, more if needed	14 oz

INGREDIENTS

potatoes

chives

unsalted butter   dried yeast

unbleached strong white flour

sugar

ORDER OF WORK

1 **PREPARE THE POTATOES AND MAKE THE DOUGH**

2 **KNEAD THE DOUGH AND LET IT RISE**

3 **SHAPE AND BAKE THE LOAF**

1 PREPARE THE POTATOES AND MAKE THE DOUGH

1 Peel the potatoes and cut them into 2–3 pieces. Put them in the saucepan with plenty of cold water, cover, and bring to a boil. Simmer just until they are tender when pierced with the tip of a knife, 15–20 minutes.

2 Drain the potatoes; reserve 250 ml (8 fl oz) of the cooking liquid. Mash the potatoes with the potato masher. There should be 175 ml (6 fl oz) mashed potato. Let the reserved liquid and potatoes cool.

3 In a small bowl, sprinkle or crumble the yeast over the water. Let stand until dissolved, stirring once, about 5 minutes.

4 Melt half of the butter in the saucepan. Meanwhile, finely chop the chives.

ANNE SAYS
"Wash and dry the chives before chopping only if they are dirty."

5 Put the reserved potato liquid, mashed potato, dissolved yeast, and melted butter into a large bowl. Add the chopped chives, sugar, and salt and mix with your hand.

6 Stir in half of the flour and mix well with your hand. Add the remaining flour, 60 g (2 oz) at a time, mixing well after each addition. Keep adding flour until the dough pulls away from the side of the bowl in a ball. It should be soft and slightly sticky.

2 KNEAD THE DOUGH AND LET IT RISE

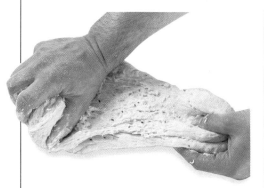  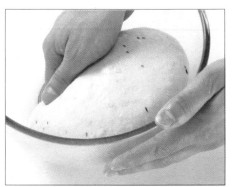

1 Turn the dough onto a floured work surface. Sprinkle the dough and your hands with flour, and begin to knead by holding the dough with one hand and pushing it away from you with the other.

2 Continue to knead by peeling the dough from the surface. Give the dough a quarter turn, and knead until it is very smooth, elastic, and forms a ball, 5–7 minutes. If the dough sticks while kneading, flour the work surface.

3 Wash the large bowl and brush it with melted butter. Put the kneaded dough in the bowl, and flip it so the surface is lightly buttered. Cover the bowl with a damp tea towel and let the dough rise in a warm place until doubled in bulk, 1–1½ hours.

3 SHAPE AND BAKE THE LOAF

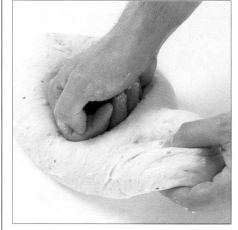

1 Brush the ring mould with melted butter. Melt the remaining 60 g (2 oz) butter and pour it into the shallow dish. Turn the dough onto a lightly floured work surface and knead with your hand just to knock out the air, 15–20 seconds. Cover the dough and let rest, about 5 minutes.

2 Flour your hands and pinch off walnut-sized pieces of dough, making about 30 pieces.

Roll dough firmly for tight, round balls

Hands should be floured for shaping balls, because dough may be quite sticky

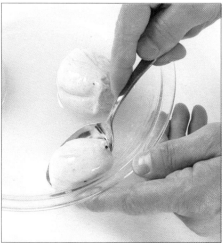

3 Roll each piece of dough between the palms of your hands to shape into smooth balls.

4 Put a few balls of dough into the dish of melted butter and turn them with a spoon until coated.

5 Transfer the balls of dough to the prepared mould. Repeat with the remaining dough. Cover the mould with a dry tea towel, and let the loaf rise in a warm place until the mould is full, about 40 minutes.

Use spoon to drop buttered balls of dough into mould

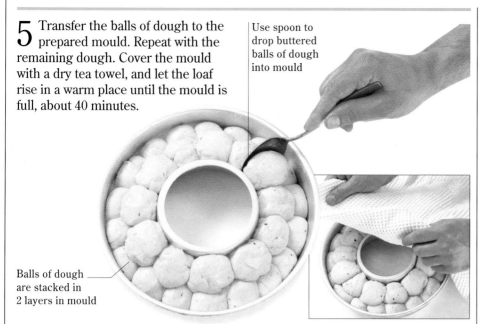

Balls of dough are stacked in 2 layers in mould

6 Heat the oven to 190°C (375°F, Gas 5). Bake the loaf in the heated oven until golden brown and the bread starts to shrink from the side of the mould, 40–45 minutes. Let cool slightly on the wire rack, then carefully unmould.

🍽 **TO SERVE**
With your fingers or 2 forks, pull the bread apart while still warm. It is delicious with roast chicken.

Chives add specks of colour and flavour to bread

Monkey bread pulls apart into rolls

VARIATION

SOURED CREAM AND DILL POTATO BREAD

Here, potato bread is flavoured with soured cream and fresh dill.

1 Omit the melted butter for coating, and omit the chives. Strip the leaves from 5–7 sprigs of fresh dill, and coarsely chop them.
2 Prepare the potatoes and make the dough, using 60 g (2 oz) butter and adding the dill in place of the chives. Knead, and let rise as directed.
3 Brush a ring mould with melted butter. Put 75 ml (2½ fl oz) soured cream into a small bowl in place of the melted butter for coating. Knock the air out of the dough, and let rest as directed. Cut the dough in half. With your hands, roll the pieces of dough into cylinders about 5 cm (2 inches) in diameter. Cut each cylinder into 4 equal pieces.
4 Lightly flour the work surface. Cup a piece of dough under the palm of your hand and roll the dough in a circular motion so it forms a smooth ball. Drop the ball of dough into the mould. Brush the sides and top of the ball of dough with the soured cream. Repeat with the remaining dough, arranging the balls evenly in the mould.
5 Let the loaf rise as directed. Heat the oven to 190°C (375°F, Gas 5). Bake, cool, and unmould the bread as directed.

SESAME BREADSTICKS

Grissini Siciliani

🍽 MAKES 32   🥣 WORK TIME 40–45 MINUTES*   🍲 BAKING TIME 15–18 MINUTES

EQUIPMENT

rolling pin

3 baking sheets

bowls

wire rack

tea towels

chef's knife

pastry brush

pastry scraper

ANNE SAYS
"*You can make and knead the dough in a heavy-duty electric mixer fitted with a dough hook, or in a food processor.*"

Tradition has it that breadsticks should be pulled to the length of the baker's outstretched arms, though these sticks are a bit shorter than that. In the Sicilian style, sesame seeds are sprinkled on top.

GETTING AHEAD
Breadsticks can be kept up to 1 week in an airtight container.
plus 1–1½ hours rising time

metric	SHOPPING LIST	imperial
12.5 ml	dried yeast, or 15 g (½ oz) fresh yeast	2½ tsp
300 ml	lukewarm water	½ pint
425 g	unbleached strong white flour, more if needed	14 oz
15 ml	sugar	1 tbsp
10 ml	salt	2 tsp
30 ml	olive oil,	2 tbsp
	more for brushing dough and baking sheets	
45 g	sesame seeds	1½ oz

INGREDIENTS

olive oil

sesame seeds

dried yeast

unbleached strong white flour

sugar

ORDER OF WORK

1 MAKE AND KNEAD THE DOUGH, AND LET IT RISE

2 CUT AND BAKE THE BREADSTICKS

1 MAKE AND KNEAD THE DOUGH, AND LET IT RISE

1 In a small bowl, sprinkle or crumble the yeast over 60 ml (4 tbsp) of the water. Let stand until dissolved, stirring once, about 5 minutes.

Wall of flour should be uniform in thickness

Well made in centre holds liquid ingredients

2 Put the flour onto a work surface with the sugar and salt. Make a large well in the centre and add the dissolved yeast, remaining water, and the oil.

3 With your fingertips, work the ingredients in the well until thoroughly mixed. Begin to draw in the flour.

4 Continue to draw in the flour with the pastry scraper and work it into the other ingredients with your hand to form a smooth dough. It should be soft and slightly sticky.

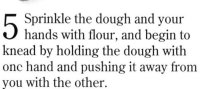

If necessary, gradually work in more flour while kneading

5 Sprinkle the dough and your hands with flour, and begin to knead by holding the dough with one hand and pushing it away from you with the other.

ANNE SAYS
"*Kneading is easy and more effective when you develop a regular, rhythmic action for pushing, peeling back, and turning the dough.*"

6 Continue to knead by peeling the dough from the surface. Give the dough a quarter turn, and knead until it is very smooth, elastic, and forms a ball, 5–7 minutes. If the dough sticks while kneading, flour the work surface.

7 Cover the dough with a damp tea towel, and let rest, about 5 minutes. Flour your hands and pat the dough into a rectangle on a well-floured work surface.

Once rested, dough does not resist patting and stretching

8 With the rolling pin, roll the dough to a 40 x 15 cm (16 x 6 inch) rectangle, pressing evenly so that the breadsticks will be uniform in thickness. Brush the dough lightly with oil.

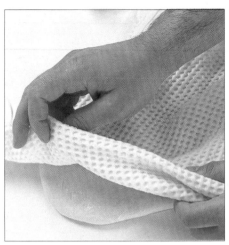

9 Cover the dough with the damp tea towel, and let rise until doubled in bulk, 1–1½ hours. Rising time will depend on the temperature of the room.

2 CUT AND BAKE THE BREADSTICKS

1 Heat the oven to 220°C (425°F, Gas 7). Brush the baking sheets with oil. Gently lift the dough to prevent it from sticking to the work surface. Lightly brush the dough with water.

2 Sprinkle the dough with the sesame seeds, and press them down gently into the surface of the dough.

3 With the chef's knife, cut the dough across into 32 strips, each about 1.25 cm (½ inch) wide.

Use whole length of knife blade to cut dough

ANNE SAYS
"The dough is not left to rise after the breadsticks are cut."

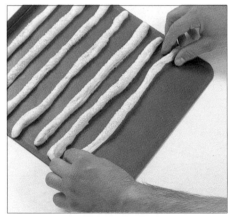

4 Stretch 1 strip of dough to the width of a baking sheet. Set it on 1 of the prepared baking sheets, letting the dough come just to the edges. Repeat to stretch the remaining strips, arranging them 2 cm (¾ inch) apart on the baking sheets.

5 Bake the breadsticks in the heated oven, 2 baking sheets at a time, until golden and crisp, 15–18 minutes. Transfer the breadsticks to the wire rack and let cool completely.

ANNE SAYS
"Keep the third sheet of unbaked breadsticks in the refrigerator until there is room to bake them in the oven."

TO SERVE
Serve breadsticks with drinks, and with cold or warm antipasti.

Breadsticks are crisp and crunchy

VARIATION
SPANISH BREAD LOOPS

Known as picos, *these crisp treats are made by tying strips of dough in loops. Coarse salt is sprinkled on top for flavour. The bread loops can be kept up to 1 week in an airtight container*

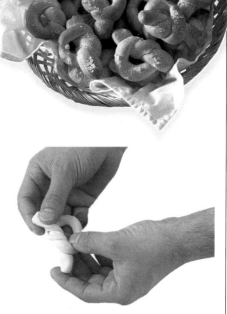

1 Omit the sesame seeds. Make half of the dough, using 6.25 ml (1 1/4 tsp) dried yeast, or 8 g (1/4 oz) fresh yeast, 150 ml (5 fl oz) lukewarm water, 225 g (7 1/2 oz) unbleached strong white flour, 7.5 ml (1 1/2 tsp) sugar, 2.5 ml (1/2 tsp) salt, and 15 ml (1 tbsp) olive oil.
2 Knead the dough, and let rest as directed. Roll it to a 20 x 15 cm (8 x 6 inch) rectangle. Cover the dough, and let rise as directed.

3 Heat the oven to 220°C (425°F, Gas 7). Brush 2 baking sheets with oil. Cut the dough across into 16 strips, then cut each dough strip in half.
4 Loop each strip, twisting the ends in a single knot. Transfer to a prepared baking sheet, and repeat to shape the remaining strips.
5 Lightly brush the loops with water and sprinkle with 22.5 ml (1 1/2 tbsp) coarse salt. Bake the loops until golden and crisp, 18–20 minutes. Let the loops cool as directed.

Sesame seeds are a savoury garnish for breadsticks

PESTO GARLAND BREAD

🍴🍽 MAKES 1 MEDIUM LOAF   🥣 WORK TIME 35–40 MINUTES*   ♨ BAKING TIME 30–35 MINUTES

EQUIPMENT

- bowls
- food processor†
- paper towels
- wire rack
- pastry brush
- rubber spatula
- chef's knife
- pepper mill
- rolling pin
- baking sheet
- tea towels
- chopping board

†blender can also be used for making pesto

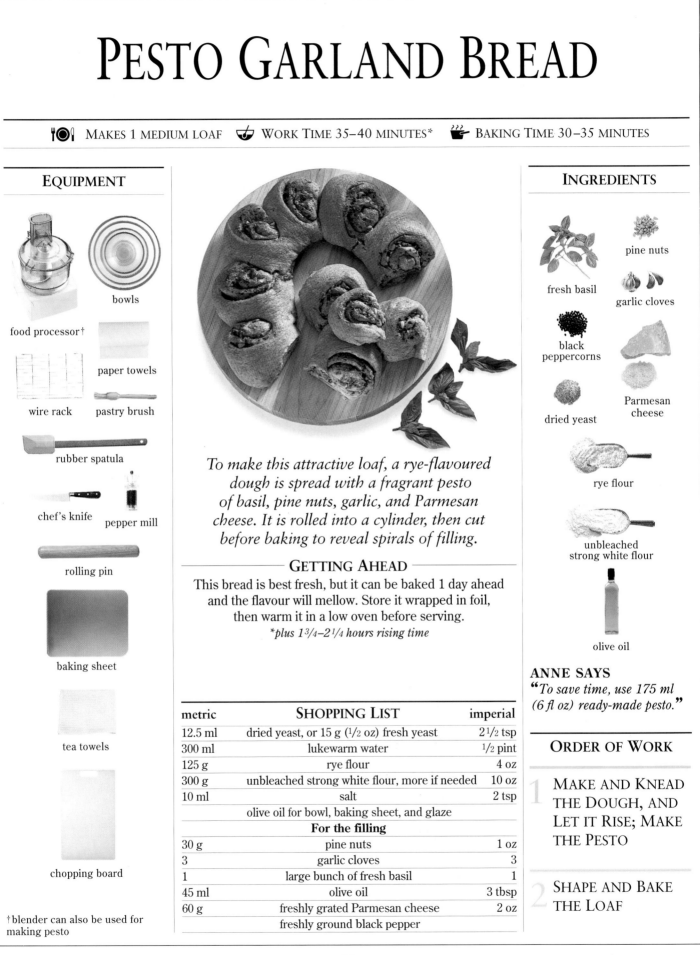

INGREDIENTS

- fresh basil
- pine nuts
- garlic cloves
- black peppercorns
- Parmesan cheese
- dried yeast
- rye flour
- unbleached strong white flour
- olive oil

To make this attractive loaf, a rye-flavoured dough is spread with a fragrant pesto of basil, pine nuts, garlic, and Parmesan cheese. It is rolled into a cylinder, then cut before baking to reveal spirals of filling.

GETTING AHEAD
This bread is best fresh, but it can be baked 1 day ahead and the flavour will mellow. Store it wrapped in foil, then warm it in a low oven before serving.
plus 1³/₄–2¹/₄ hours rising time

ANNE SAYS
"To save time, use 175 ml (6 fl oz) ready-made pesto."

ORDER OF WORK

1 MAKE AND KNEAD THE DOUGH, AND LET IT RISE; MAKE THE PESTO

2 SHAPE AND BAKE THE LOAF

metric	SHOPPING LIST	imperial
12.5 ml	dried yeast, or 15 g (¹/₂ oz) fresh yeast	2¹/₂ tsp
300 ml	lukewarm water	¹/₂ pint
125 g	rye flour	4 oz
300 g	unbleached strong white flour, more if needed	10 oz
10 ml	salt	2 tsp
	olive oil for bowl, baking sheet, and glaze	
	For the filling	
30 g	pine nuts	1 oz
3	garlic cloves	3
1	large bunch of fresh basil	1
45 ml	olive oil	3 tbsp
60 g	freshly grated Parmesan cheese	2 oz
	freshly ground black pepper	

1 MAKE AND KNEAD THE DOUGH, AND LET IT RISE; MAKE THE PESTO

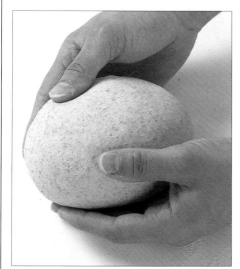

1 Make and knead the dough in the food processor (see box, page 64).

ANNE SAYS
"If you like, you can make and knead the dough by hand. Start with the liquid ingredients in a large bowl, then add the dry ingredients."

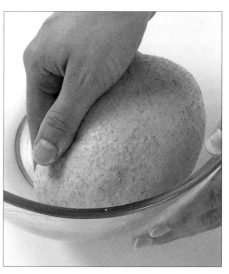

2 Brush a large bowl with oil. Put the dough in the bowl, and flip it so it is lightly oiled. Cover the bowl with a damp tea towel and let the dough rise in a warm place until doubled in bulk, 1–1½ hours.

3 With the chef's knife, coarsely chop the pine nuts. Set the flat side of the chef's knife on top of each garlic clove and strike it with your fist. Discard the skin.

ANNE SAYS
"Garlic cloves are crushed to remove skin easily."

Weight and width of knife blade makes crushing garlic easy

4 Strip the basil leaves from the stalks. Rinse the leaves, drain them on paper towels, and put them in the food processor or blender with the garlic cloves.

Basil leaves must be dry so pesto is not watery

Pungent garlic and aromatic basil form base of pesto

5 Work the mixture until coarsely chopped. With the blades turning, gradually add the olive oil and work until smooth. Scrape down the side of the bowl from time to time with the rubber spatula.

How to Make and Knead Dough in a Food Processor

The food processor is a fast alternative to making and kneading dough by hand. Standard food processors fitted with a steel blade are suitable for kneading doughs made with no more than 425 g (14 oz) flour, therefore the processor is suggested for small quantities only. If you have a large machine, you may use the plastic dough blade to knead larger quantities.

2 Put the rye flour and half of the strong white flour in the work bowl with the salt. Combine the dissolved yeast and remaining water and pour in, working with the pulse button just until mixed.

ANNE SAYS
"*This dough-making method can be used in a variety of recipes, using dry and liquid ingredients as specified.*"

1 In a small bowl, sprinkle or crumble the yeast over 60 ml (4 tbsp) of the water. Let stand until dissolved, stirring once, about 5 minutes.

3 Add the remaining flour, 60 g (2 oz) at a time. Work each addition until mixed. Keep adding flour until the dough pulls away from the side of the bowl in a ball. It should be soft and slightly sticky.

Work in each batch of flour before adding more

4 Continue working the dough in the food processor until it is very smooth and elastic, 60 seconds longer. Turn the dough onto a lightly floured work surface and remove the blade. Shape the dough into a ball.

! TAKE CARE !
If the food processor slows down and the motor begins to strain, turn it off. Continue kneading the dough by hand.

Pesto ingredients
come together
easily

Pine nuts
add texture
to mixture

6 Transfer the pesto
mixture to a bowl
and stir in the pine
nuts, Parmesan cheese,
and plenty of black pepper.
Taste for seasoning.

! TAKE CARE !
*The Parmesan cheese is salty, so you
may not need any salt.*

2 SHAPE AND BAKE THE LOAF

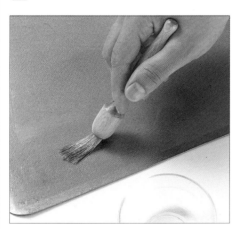

1 Brush the baking sheet with oil.
Turn the dough onto a lightly
floured work surface and knead with
your hand just to knock out the air,
15–20 seconds. Cover the dough,
and let rest, about 5 minutes.

2 Flatten the dough with
the palms of your hands,
then roll it into a 40 x 30 cm
(16 x 12 inch) rectangle with
the rolling pin. Use your hands
to shape the rectangle.

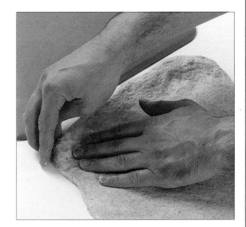

Apply gentle
pressure with
spatula to spread
pesto evenly

3 With the rubber spatula, spread the
pesto filling evenly over the dough,
leaving a 1.25 cm (½ inch) border.

Border is left so
dough rolls into
cylinder easily

4 Starting with a long end, roll up the rectangle into a cylinder, keeping the cylinder even from middle to end.

Fingers are perfect for pinching seam

5 Running the length of the cylinder, pinch the seam firmly together. Do not seal the ends.

ANNE SAYS
"This is a moist dough. The seam seals easily."

Centre ring on baking sheet

6 Transfer the cylinder seam-side down to the prepared baking sheet. Curve the cylinder into a ring, overlapping and sealing the ends.

Press and pinch ends together to seal ring

7 With the chef's knife, make a series of deep cuts around the ring, about 5 cm (2 inches) apart.

! TAKE CARE !
Do not cut completely through the ring.

8 Pull the slices apart slightly and twist them over to lie flat. Cover with a dry tea towel and let the loaf rise in a warm place until doubled in bulk, about 45 minutes.

9 Heat the oven to 220°C (425°F, Gas 7). Brush the loaf with oil and bake in the heated oven, 10 minutes. Reduce the heat to 190°C (375°F, Gas 5) and continue baking until well browned, 20–25 minutes longer.

10 Carefully transfer the bread from the baking sheet to the wire rack and let cool slightly.

Slide bread gently onto rack

🍽 **TO SERVE**
Serve this bread, as an accompaniment to pasta or a salad of ripe tomatoes.

Spiral exposes savoury filling

Garland is sliced or broken into pieces

V A R I A T I O N

SUN-DRIED TOMATO SPIRAL

Sun-dried tomatoes make a gutsy filling for this spiral loaf.

1 Make the dough, and let it rise.
2 Drain 75 g (2½ oz) oil-packed sun-dried tomatoes, reserving 30 ml (2 tbsp) of the oil; coarsely chop. Chop the pine nuts. Peel and chop 2 garlic cloves. Strip the leaves from 5–10 sprigs of fresh basil and finely chop them.
3 Put the sun-dried tomatoes in a small bowl with the pine nuts, garlic, basil, and the grated Parmesan cheese. Stir in 15 ml (1 tbsp) reserved oil and season with plenty of black pepper.
4 Brush an 20 cm (8 inch) round cake tin with the remaining oil. Sprinkle 15–30 ml (1–2 tbsp) polenta in the tin and turn it to coat the bottom and side; turn the tin upside down and tap to remove excess cornmeal. Knock the air out of the dough and let rest as directed. Roll the dough into a rectangle, spread the filling, and shape a cylinder.
5 Flip the cylinder so it is seam-side down, curve it around into a spiral, and tuck the end underneath. Drop it into the tin, cover, and let rise as directed. Bake the loaf as directed, allowing 25–30 minutes at 190°C (375°F, Gas 5). Unmould and let cool.

SPICED LAMB PIES

🍽 MAKES 12   🥣 WORK TIME 40–45 MINUTES*   ♨ BAKING TIME 10–15 MINUTES

EQUIPMENT

chef's knife

pastry brush

small knife

large sauté pan with lid†

saucepan

bowls

tea towels

2 baking sheets

chopping board

wooden spoon

slotted spoon

rolling pin

†frying pan can also be used

ANNE SAYS

"You can make and knead the dough in a heavy-duty electric mixer fitted with a dough hook, or in a food processor."

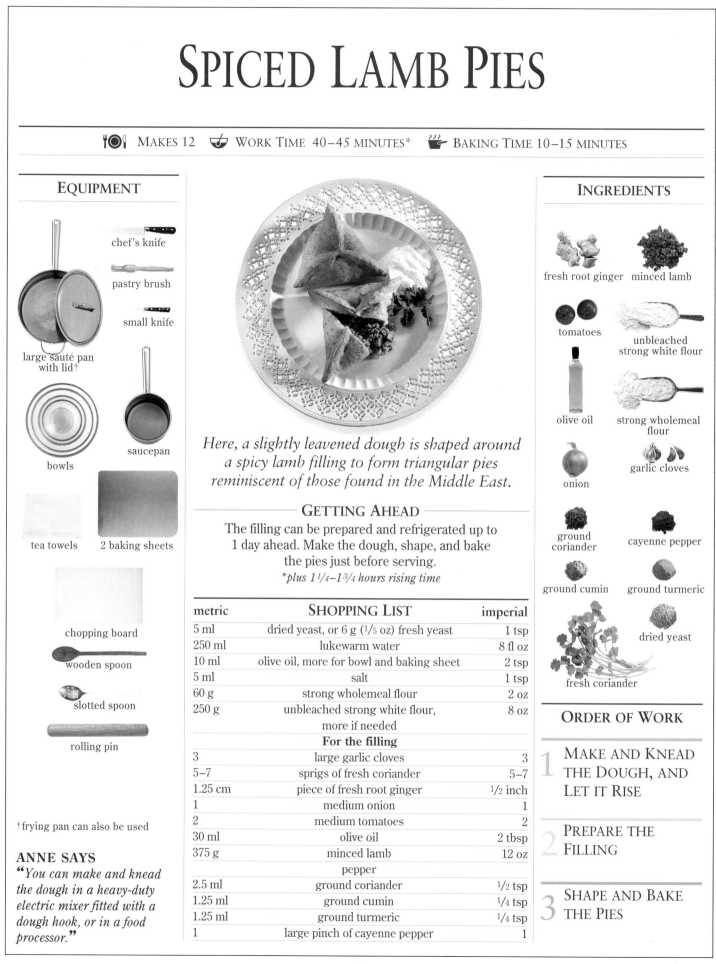

Here, a slightly leavened dough is shaped around a spicy lamb filling to form triangular pies reminiscent of those found in the Middle East.

GETTING AHEAD

The filling can be prepared and refrigerated up to 1 day ahead. Make the dough, shape, and bake the pies just before serving.

*plus 1 1/4–1 3/4 hours rising time

metric	SHOPPING LIST	imperial
5 ml	dried yeast, or 6 g (1/5 oz) fresh yeast	1 tsp
250 ml	lukewarm water	8 fl oz
10 ml	olive oil, more for bowl and baking sheet	2 tsp
5 ml	salt	1 tsp
60 g	strong wholemeal flour	2 oz
250 g	unbleached strong white flour, more if needed	8 oz
For the filling		
3	large garlic cloves	3
5–7	sprigs of fresh coriander	5–7
1.25 cm	piece of fresh root ginger	1/2 inch
1	medium onion	1
2	medium tomatoes	2
30 ml	olive oil	2 tbsp
375 g	minced lamb	12 oz
	pepper	
2.5 ml	ground coriander	1/2 tsp
1.25 ml	ground cumin	1/4 tsp
1.25 ml	ground turmeric	1/4 tsp
1	large pinch of cayenne pepper	1

INGREDIENTS

fresh root ginger   minced lamb

tomatoes

unbleached strong white flour

olive oil

strong wholemeal flour

garlic cloves

onion

ground coriander

cayenne pepper

ground cumin

ground turmeric

dried yeast

fresh coriander

ORDER OF WORK

1 MAKE AND KNEAD THE DOUGH, AND LET IT RISE

2 PREPARE THE FILLING

3 SHAPE AND BAKE THE PIES

1 MAKE AND KNEAD THE DOUGH, AND LET IT RISE

1 In a small bowl, sprinkle or crumble the yeast over 60 ml (4 tbsp) of the water. Let stand until dissolved, stirring once, about 5 minutes.

2 Put the dissolved yeast, remaining water, oil, and salt in a large bowl. Stir in the wholemeal flour with half of the strong white flour and mix well with your hand.

3 Add the remaining strong white flour, 60 g (2 oz) at a time, mixing well after each addition. Keep adding flour until the dough pulls away from the side of the bowl in a ball. It should be soft and slightly sticky. Turn the dough onto a floured work surface, and knead by hand (see box, below).

HOW TO KNEAD DOUGH BY HAND

Kneading is important in bread making because it distributes the yeast, and develops the gluten. Gluten holds the gas bubbles produced by the yeast and gives elasticity to bread dough. Kneading also gives bread an even texture. The amount of flour the dough absorbs while kneading and the time it takes to knead vary with each recipe.

1 Holding the dough with one hand, press firmly down into the dough with the heel of your other hand, pushing the dough away from you.

2 Peel the dough back from the work surface in one piece, fold it over, and give it a quarter turn.

Hands and work surface should be lightly floured

3 Continue kneading the dough in this way, pushing it away from you, peeling, and turning it. The kneaded dough should be very smooth, elastic, and in the form of a ball. If the dough sticks while kneading, flour the work surface.

4 Press the dough with your finger. The dough will spring back when it has been sufficiently kneaded.

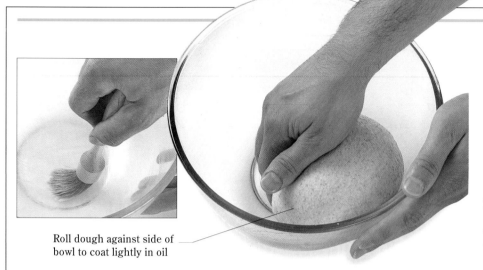

Roll dough against side of bowl to coat lightly in oil

4 Wash the large bowl and brush it with oil. Put the kneaded dough in the bowl, and flip it so the surface is lightly oiled. Cover the bowl with a damp tea towel and let the dough rise in a warm place until doubled in bulk, 1–1½ hours. Prepare the filling.

ANNE SAYS
"The speed at which the dough rises depends largely on its temperature – the warmer it is, the quicker it rises."

2 PREPARE THE FILLING

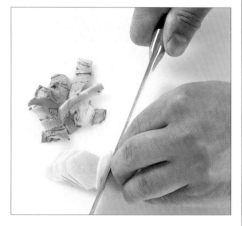

1 Set the flat side of the chef's knife on top of each garlic clove and strike it with your fist. Discard the skin and finely chop the cloves.

2 Strip the coriander leaves from the stalks and pile them on the chopping board. With the chef's knife, finely chop the leaves.

3 With the small knife, peel the skin from the root ginger. With the chef's knife, slice the ginger, cutting across the fibrous grain. Crush each slice with the flat of the knife, then finely chop the slices.

ANNE SAYS
"Mature ginger is usually peeled before use. Young ginger, pink in colour and less pungent in flavour, does not have a tough skin and can be used without peeling."

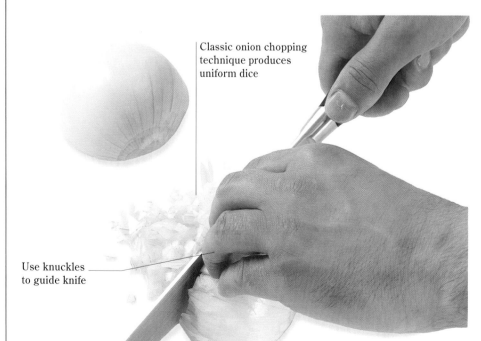

Classic onion chopping technique produces uniform dice

Use knuckles to guide knife

4 Peel the onion, leaving a little of the root attached, and cut it lengthways in half. Lay each onion half flat on the chopping board and slice horizontally towards the root, leaving the slices attached at the root end. Then slice vertically, again leaving the root end uncut. Finally, cut across the onion to make dice.

Tomatoes are scored before blanching to make peeling easy

5 Cut out the cores, and score an "x" on the base of each tomato. Immerse the tomatoes in a saucepan of boiling water until the skins start to split, 8–15 seconds, depending on their ripeness. With the slotted spoon, transfer the tomatoes at once to a bowl of cold water. When cool, peel off the skins. Cut the tomatoes crossways in half, squeeze out the seeds, then coarsely chop each half.

6 Heat the oil in the sauté pan. Add the lamb, season with salt and pepper, and cook over medium-high heat, stirring often to break up the meat, until it is evenly browned, 5–7 minutes. With the slotted spoon transfer the lamb to a bowl. Reduce the heat to medium and pour off all but 30 ml (2 tbsp) of the fat.

7 Add the garlic and ginger to the pan and fry until fragrant, 30 seconds. Add the onion and cook, stirring occasionally, until the onion is soft, 3–5 minutes.

8 Add the ground coriander, cumin, turmeric, and cayenne pepper to the pan. Add the lamb and the tomatoes, cover and cook, stirring occasionally, until thickened, about 10 minutes.

Fresh coriander is added at end of cooking to preserve its delicate flavour

9 Remove the pan from the heat. Stir in the chopped coriander and taste for seasoning. Let the filling

ANNE SAYS
"*Taste the lamb mixture again once it has cooled. It should be well seasoned.*"

Lamb filling is aromatic with spices

2 Shape and Bake the Pies

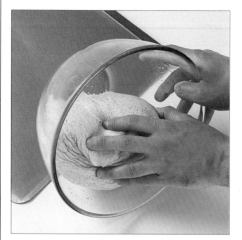

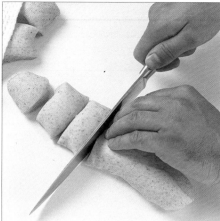

Rested dough is easy to roll

1 Brush the baking sheets with oil. Turn the dough onto a lightly floured work surface and knead with your hand just to knock out the air, 15–20 seconds. Cover the dough, and let rest, about 5 minutes.

2 Cut the dough in half. With your hands, shape 1 piece of dough into a cylinder about 5 cm (2 inches) in diameter. Cut the cylinder into 6 pieces, and cover them. Repeat to shape and divide the remaining dough.

3 Shape a piece of dough into a ball. With the rolling pin, roll the ball into a 10 cm (4 inch) round.

ANNE SAYS
"Be sure to keep the work surface lightly floured."

Lamb mixture is studded with onion and tomato

Use 1–2 tbsp of lamb mixture to fill each pie

4 Spoon some of the lamb filling into the centre of the round, leaving a 2.5 cm (1 inch) border of dough.

! TAKE CARE !
Work quickly to keep the dough from drying out.

5 With your fingers, lift the dough up and over the lamb filling to form a triangular parcel.

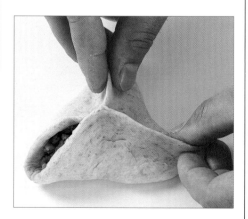

6 Pinch the edges together with your fingers to seal. Place the pie on a prepared baking sheet. Repeat to shape and fill the remaining dough.

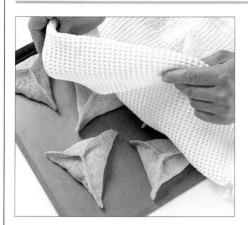

7 Cover the pies with a dry tea towel, and let rise in a warm place until puffed, about 20 minutes. Heat the oven to 230°C (450°F, Gas 8).

Handle hot pies with tea towel

8 Bake the pies in the heated oven until the bottoms are golden brown, 10–15 minutes.

Well-baked pies are nicely browned

⑪ TO SERVE
Serve the pies warm from the oven with a spoonful or two of plain yogurt.

Golden pastry wraps around aromatic lamb and tomato filling

PITA BREAD

This pocket bread is delicious completely plain or stuffed with salad. I sometimes add cumin seeds to the dough, as suggested here.

1 Omit the lamb filling. Make the dough, adding 10 ml (2 tsp) cumin seeds with the flour. Knead the dough, and let rise as directed.
2 Generously flour 2 baking sheets. Knock the air out of the dough and let rest as directed. Shape the dough into a cylinder about 5 cm (2 inches) wide, then cut the cylinder into 6 pieces. Shape 1 piece of dough into a ball, then roll the ball into an 18 cm (7 inch) round. Transfer the round to a prepared baking sheet. Repeat to shape the remaining dough. Cover the dough, and let rise as directed.
3 Heat the oven to its maximum setting. Put an additional baking sheet in the oven to heat. With a palette knife, gently loosen the rounds from 1 of the baking sheets. Slide the loosened rounds all at once onto the heated baking sheet and bake them in the oven until puffed, about 5 minutes.
4 Transfer the breads to a wire rack and brush the tops lightly with water. Bake the remaining rounds. Brush any excess flour off the bottom of each pita and serve while still warm. Makes 6 pita breads.

RED ONION CONFIT AND GORGONZOLA PIZZAS

🍴 MAKES 6   🥄 WORK TIME 40–45 MINUTES*   🍲 BAKING TIME 15–20 MINUTES

EQUIPMENT

wooden spoon

chef's knife

pastry brush

medium frying pan with lid

tea towels

pastry scraper

bowls

chopping board

aluminum foil

rolling pin

2 baking sheets

Onions and Gorgonzola are delicious together, here topping a crust made crunchy with polenta. To make confit, sliced red onions are cooked very slowly to soften in their own juices, with red wine added for colour.

GETTING AHEAD

The onion confit can be made 1 day ahead and kept, covered, in the refrigerator. The pizza dough can be made, kneaded, and left in the refrigerator to rise overnight. Shape the dough and let it come to room temperature. Assemble and bake the pizzas just before serving.
*plus 1¼–1¾ hours rising time

metric	SHOPPING LIST	imperial
7.5 ml	dried yeast, or 10 g (⅓ oz) fresh yeast	1½ tsp
250 ml	lukewarm water	8 fl oz
250 g	unbleached strong white flour, more if needed	8 oz
75 g	polenta (fine yellow cornmeal), more for squares of foil	2½ oz
5 ml	salt	1 tsp
30 ml	olive oil, more for bowl and serving	2 tbsp
	For the topping	
750 g	red onions	1½ lb
30 ml	olive oil	2 tbsp
10 ml	sugar	2 tsp
	pepper	
60 ml	red wine	4 tbsp
5–7	sprigs of fresh oregano	5–7
175 g	Gorgonzola cheese	6 oz

INGREDIENTS

red onions

Gorgonzola cheese†

red wine

olive oil

dried yeast

polenta

fresh oregano

unbleached strong white flour

sugar

†Roquefort cheese can also be used

ORDER OF WORK

1 MAKE AND KNEAD THE DOUGH, AND LET IT RISE

2 MAKE THE ONION CONFIT

3 ASSEMBLE AND BAKE THE PIZZAS

1 MAKE AND KNEAD THE DOUGH, AND LET IT RISE

1 In a small bowl, sprinkle or crumble the yeast over 60 ml (4 tbsp) of the water. Let stand until dissolved, stirring once, about 5 minutes.

2 Put the flour onto the work surface with the polenta and salt. Make a large well in the centre and add the remaining water, the oil, and dissolved yeast.

3 With your fingertips, work the ingredients in the well until thoroughly mixed. Begin to draw in the flour mixture.

Draw flour into liquid ingredients without breaking through side of well

4 Continue to draw in flour with the pastry scraper and work it into the other ingredients with your hand to form a smooth dough. It should be soft and slightly sticky.

ANNE SAYS
"If necessary, work in more flour while kneading the dough."

5 Sprinkle the dough and your hands with flour, and begin to knead by holding the dough with one hand and pushing it away from you with the other.

ANNE SAYS
"Kneading is easy and more effective when you develop a regular, rhythmic action for pushing, peeling back, and turning the dough."

Push dough firmly against floured work surface

Kneading and stretching develops gluten, helping dough to rise

6 Continue to knead by peeling the dough from the surface. Give the dough a quarter turn, and knead until it is very smooth, elastic, and forms a ball, 5–7 minutes. If the dough sticks while kneading, flour the work surface.

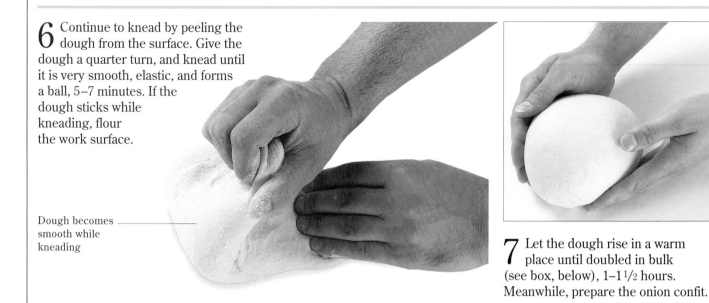

Dough becomes smooth while kneading

7 Let the dough rise in a warm place until doubled in bulk (see box, below), 1–1¹/₂ hours. Meanwhile, prepare the onion confit.

HOW TO LET DOUGH RISE

Once activated, yeast grows, causing dough to rise. The speed at which dough rises is largely controlled by temperature. In a warm place, such as an oven warmed just by the pilot light, or an electric oven with the oven light turned on, dough rises quickly. At room temperature, or in a refrigerator, dough rises at a slower rate. Dough is normally left to rise twice, after kneading, and after it has been shaped. The flavour of the dough also develops as it rises. Rising time varies with the type of dough, and is indicated in each recipe.

1 Brush a large bowl with oil or melted butter.

2 Put the kneaded dough in the bowl, and flip it so its surface is covered lightly with the oil or butter.

4 To test the dough, press it gently, but firmly, with your forefinger. If the dough holds the impression of your finger, it has risen sufficiently.

! TAKE CARE !
When dough is left to rise too long, bubbles start to break on the surface, causing its eventual collapse.

3 To prevent the dough from drying out, cover the bowl with a damp tea towel, or with cling film, and let it rise in a warm place, about 30°C (85°F), until doubled in bulk.

Risen dough holds impression of forefinger

2 MAKE THE ONION CONFIT

Use knuckles to guide knife

1 Peel the onions, leaving a little of the root attached, then cut them lengthways in half. Lay each onion half flat on a chopping board and cut across into thin, even slices.

2 Heat the oil in the frying pan. Add the onions, sugar, salt, and pepper. Cook over medium heat, stirring often, until the onions are soft and lightly brown, 5–7 minutes.

3 Add the wine to the onions and continue cooking until the wine has evaporated, 1–2 minutes longer. Lower the heat, press a piece of foil on top of the onions, and cover with the lid.

4 Cook the onions over very low heat, stirring occasionally, until they are soft enough to cut with a spoon, 15–20 minutes. Let cool.

Rock chef's knife from tip to heel of blade to chop herbs efficiently

Sharp chef's knife makes easy work of chopping herbs

5 Strip the oregano leaves from the stalks, reserving 6 sprigs for decoration. Pile the leaves on the chopping board and finely chop them with the chef's knife. Stir the chopped oregano into the onion confit.

ANNE SAYS
"If you prefer, choose your favourite herb; fresh basil, sage, thyme, or marjoram all work well here."

3 ASSEMBLE AND BAKE THE PIZZAS

1 Heat the oven to 230°C (450°F, Gas 8). Put the baking sheets on separate racks in the bottom half of the oven to heat. Cut six 23 cm (9 inch) squares of foil, and sprinkle each square generously with polenta.

2 Turn the dough onto a lightly floured work surface and knead with your hand just to knock out the air, 15–20 seconds. Cover the dough, and let rest, about 5 minutes.

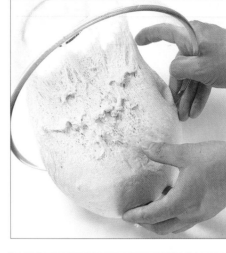

Dough is rolled into cylinder so it can be divided easily

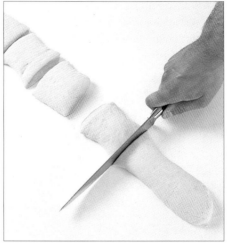

3 With your hands, roll the dough into a cylinder about 5 cm (2 inches) in diameter.

4 With the chef's knife, cut the cylinder in half, and then cut each half into 3 equal pieces.

5 Shape the pieces of dough into balls: cup a piece of dough under the palm of your hand, and roll it in a circular motion.

6 Roll a ball of dough into an 18 cm (7 inch) round. Transfer the round to 1 of the squares of prepared foil. Repeat to shape the remaining dough.

7 Press up the edges of the rounds with your fingertips to form shallow rims. Spread the rounds with the onion confit.

8 Top the rounds with cheese, and let rise in a warm place until the dough is puffed, about 15 minutes. Bake the pizzas, on the foil, on the baking sheets, until lightly browned and crisp, 15–20 minutes. Switch the baking sheets after 7 minutes so the pizzas brown evenly.

ANNE SAYS
"Baking the pizzas on a hot baking sheet makes for crisp crusts. Foil makes them easy to transfer."

Gorgonzola should be soft for crumbling

TO SERVE
Serve the pizzas hot from the oven. Brush the crust with olive oil, and top with the reserved oregano sprigs.

Crust brushed with olive oil is golden and full of flavour

Pizza topping is mellow with caramelized onions and sharp with Gorgonzola

VARIATION

SPINACH AND RICOTTA PIZZAS

Here, the same pizza dough is topped with ricotta cheese, sautéed spinach, ripe plum tomatoes, olive oil, and freshly ground black pepper.

1 Omit the onions, sugar, red wine, oregano, and Gorgonzola. Make and knead the dough, and let it rise as directed. Peel and chop 2 garlic cloves. Discard the tough ribs and stalks from 750 g (1 1/2 lb) spinach, then wash the leaves in plenty of cold water. Dry the spinach well. Roll a few spinach leaves and cut across into shreds. Shred the remaining leaves.

2 Heat 30 ml (2 tbsp) olive oil in a large frying pan. Add the garlic and fry until fragrant, 30 seconds. Add the spinach, salt, and pepper, and stir. Cover the pan and cook over medium-high heat until the spinach is wilted, 3–5 minutes. Uncover and cook, stirring constantly, until any moisture evaporates, 1–2 minutes longer. Taste for seasoning and let the spinach cool. Core 5 plum tomatoes, and cut each one lengthways into 4 slices. Season 375 g (12 oz) ricotta cheese with salt and pepper.

3 Heat the oven, and heat 2 baking sheets as directed. Prepare the foil and shape the rounds. Spread the cheese on the rounds, then top each with spinach, tomato slices, 5 ml (1 tsp) olive oil, and freshly ground black pepper. Let rise, then bake as directed.

CHICAGO DEEP-DISH PIZZA

🍽 SERVES 6–8   🥣 WORK TIME 35–40 MINUTES*   🍲 BAKING TIME 20–25 MINUTES

EQUIPMENT

grater

35 cm (14 inch) deep-dish pizza pan †

small knife

chef's knife

pastry brush

medium sauté pan ‡

slotted spoon

wooden spoon

medium saucepan

baking sheet

pastry scraper

tea towels

chopping board

bowls

rolling pin

†two 23 cm (9 inch) round cake tins can also be used

‡medium frying pan can also be used

INGREDIENTS

Italian sausage

garlic cloves

dried yeast

plum tomatoes †

unbleached strong white flour

polenta

mozzarella cheese

olive oil

flat-leaf parsley ‡

†840 g (28 oz) canned plum tomatoes, drained, can also be used

‡curly parsley can also be used

ANNE SAYS
"If you prefer a spicy topping, use hot Italian sausage."

Deep-dish pizza, with its hearty crust and topping, first made its appearance in Chicago in the 1940s. Here, mild Italian sausage flavours a simple sauce of fresh tomatoes, topped with mozzarella cheese.

GETTING AHEAD

The sauce can be made 1 day ahead and kept, covered, in the refrigerator. The pizza dough can be made, kneaded, and left in the refrigerator to rise overnight. Shape the dough and let it come to room temperature. Assemble and bake the pizza just before serving.

*plus 1 1/2–2 hours rising time

metric	SHOPPING LIST	imperial
12.5 ml	dried yeast, or 15 g (1/2 oz) fresh yeast	2 1/2 tsp
300 ml	lukewarm water	1/2 pint
500 g	unbleached strong white flour, more if needed	1 lb
10 ml	salt	2 tsp
45 ml	olive oil, more for bowl and pizza pan	3 tbsp
30–45 ml	polenta (fine yellow cornmeal)	2–3 tbsp
	For the sauce	
1 kg	plum tomatoes	2 lb
3	garlic cloves	3
7–10	sprigs of flat-leaf parsley	7–10
375 g	mild Italian sausage	12 oz
15 ml	olive oil	1 tbsp
	pepper	
175 g	mozzarella cheese	6 oz

ORDER OF WORK

1. **MAKE AND KNEAD THE DOUGH, AND LET IT RISE**

2. **MAKE THE PIZZA SAUCE**

3. **ASSEMBLE AND BAKE THE PIZZA**

1 MAKE AND KNEAD THE DOUGH, AND LET IT RISE

2 Put the flour onto the work surface with the salt. Make a large well in the centre and add the dissolved yeast, remaining water, and the oil.

Wall of flour forms well for liquid ingredients

1 In a small bowl, sprinkle or crumble the yeast over 60 ml (4 tbsp) of the water. Let stand until dissolved, stirring once, about 5 minutes.

3 With your fingertips, work the liquid ingredients in the centre of the well until thoroughly and evenly mixed. Begin to draw in the flour.

4 Continue to draw in the flour with the pastry scraper and work it into the other ingredients with your hand to form a smooth dough. It should be soft and slightly sticky.

Kneading develops gluten, helping dough to rise

Dough peels from surface in one piece

5 Sprinkle the dough and your hands with flour, and begin to knead by holding the dough with one hand and pushing it away from you with the other. Continue to knead by peeling the dough from the surface. Give the dough a quarter turn and knead until it is very smooth, elastic, and forms a ball, 5–7 minutes. If the dough sticks while kneading, flour the work surface.

ANNE SAYS
"You can make and knead the dough in a heavy-duty electric mixer fitted with a dough hook."

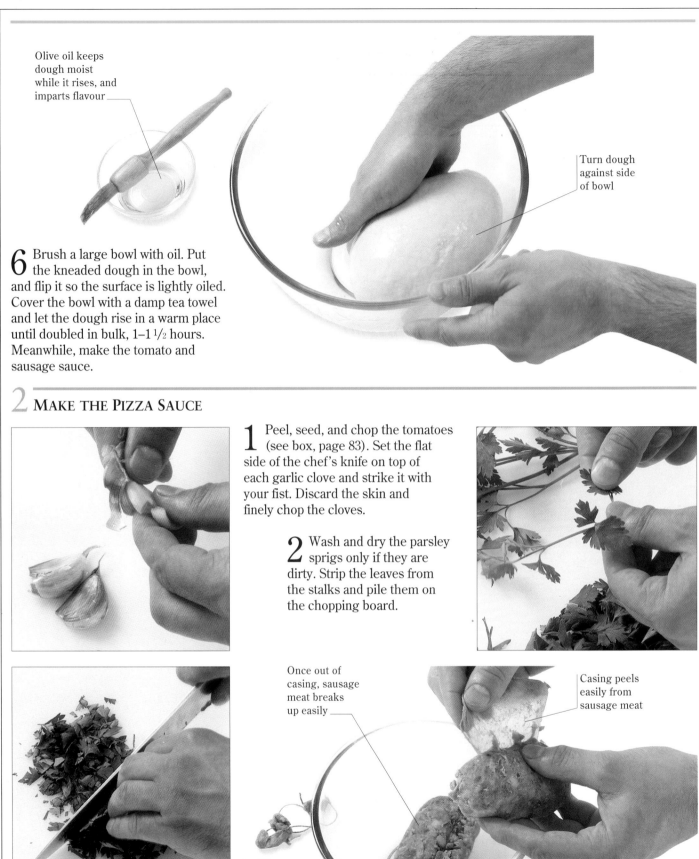

Olive oil keeps dough moist while it rises, and imparts flavour

Turn dough against side of bowl

6 Brush a large bowl with oil. Put the kneaded dough in the bowl, and flip it so the surface is lightly oiled. Cover the bowl with a damp tea towel and let the dough rise in a warm place until doubled in bulk, 1–1 ½ hours. Meanwhile, make the tomato and sausage sauce.

2 MAKE THE PIZZA SAUCE

1 Peel, seed, and chop the tomatoes (see box, page 83). Set the flat side of the chef's knife on top of each garlic clove and strike it with your fist. Discard the skin and finely chop the cloves.

2 Wash and dry the parsley sprigs only if they are dirty. Strip the leaves from the stalks and pile them on the chopping board.

Once out of casing, sausage meat breaks up easily

Casing peels easily from sausage meat

3 With the chef's knife, and using your knuckles as a guide, coarsely chop the parsley leaves.

4 Slit the side of each sausage and push out the meat, discarding the casing.

HOW TO PEEL, SEED, AND CHOP TOMATOES

Tomatoes are often peeled and seeded before chopping so that they need not be strained after cooking. The technique is the same for any variety of tomato.

1 Cut the cores from the tomatoes and score an "x" on the base of each tomato with the tip of a small knife.

2 Immerse the tomatoes in a pan of boiling water until the skins start to split, 8–15 seconds depending on their ripeness. Transfer the tomatoes at once to a bowl of cold water.

3 When the tomatoes are cool enough to handle, peel the skin off each one, using the small knife.

4 With a chef's knife, cut the tomatoes crossways in half. Squeeze out the seeds, then coarsely chop each tomato half.

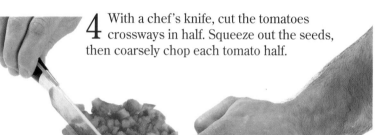

Hold tip of blade and rock handle up and down

5 Heat the oil in the sauté pan. Add the sausage meat and fry over medium-high heat, breaking up the meat with the wooden spoon, until cooked, 5–7 minutes. Reduce the heat to medium, remove the sausage meat from the pan, and pour off all but 15 ml (1 tbsp) of the fat.

Stir sausage meat for even cooking

Fat is rendered as sausage meat cooks

Mild sausage
makes savoury
and aromatic sauce

Some parsley
is reserved
for sprinkling
on top of pizza

6 Stir the garlic into the pan and fry until fragrant, about 30 seconds. Add the sausage back to the pan, and stir in the tomatoes, salt, pepper, and all but 15 ml (1 tbsp) of the parsley.

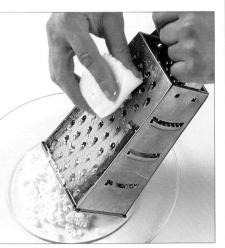

7 Cook, stirring occasionally, until the sauce is thickened, 10–15 minutes. Remove the sauce from the heat, taste for seasoning, and let cool completely. Coarsely grate the cheese.

3 ASSEMBLE AND BAKE THE PIZZA

1 Brush the pizza pan with oil. Sprinkle the polenta in the pan and turn it to coat the bottom and side; turn the pan upside down and tap to remove excess polenta.

2 Turn the dough onto a lightly floured work surface and knead with your hand just to knock out the air, 15–20 seconds. Cover, and let rest, about 5 minutes.

3 Shape the dough into a loose ball. With the rolling pin, roll the ball into a 35 cm (14 inch) round.

4 Working carefully, wrap the dough around the rolling pin and drape it over the pan.

5 With your hands, press the dough into the bottom of the pan, and 2.5 cm (1 inch) up the side to form a rim.

6 Cover the pan with a dry tea towel, and let the dough rise until puffed, about 20 minutes. Heat the oven to 230°C (450°F, Gas 8). Heat a baking sheet in the bottom third of the oven.

Sprinkling of chopped parsley is more pronounced in flavour than parsley cooked in sauce

7 Spread the sauce over the dough, leaving a 1.25 cm (½ inch) border around the edge. Sprinkle over the cheese and the remaining chopped parsley. Bake the pizza on the baking sheet in the bottom third of the heated oven until the cheese is lightly browned and the dough is crisp and golden, 20–25 minutes.

🍴 TO SERVE
Deep-dish pizza is often served from the pizza pan, but it can be taken out for easy slicing. Let the pizza cool 5 minutes, then cut it into wedges.

Thick crust and hearty topping are signatures of deep-dish pizza

PIZZA CALABRESE
Here, pizza dough is made into double-crust pies filled with artichoke hearts, black olives, and capers.

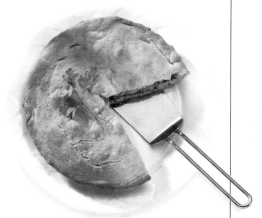

1 Make and knead the dough, and let it rise as directed. Omit the sausage and make the sauce, using all the parsley. Drain and slice 250 g (8 oz) oil-packed artichoke hearts. Pit and chop 45 g (1½ oz) oil-cured black olives. Chop 10 ml (2 tsp) drained capers. Grate the cheese.

2 Prepare two 23 cm (9 inch) round cake tins as directed. Knead the dough just to knock out the air. Cut the dough into 3 equal pieces. Shape 1 piece into a ball, then roll it to a 28 cm (11 inch) round. Drape it over 1 of the prepared tins, allowing some dough to hang over the side, and pressing the dough into the bottom of the tin. Line the second tin.

3 Spread the sauce over the dough, then top with the vegetables and cheese. Cut the remaining piece of dough in half. Roll each half to a 20 cm (8 inch) round. Drape the rounds over the filling, leaving a 2.5 cm (1 inch) border. Brush a 1.25 cm (½ inch) border of water around the edge of each round. Lift the bottom rounds of dough just to meet the top rounds, pressing gently to seal.

4 Let rise. Brush the dough with olive oil, and cut an "x" in the centre of each pie. Bake and let cool as directed.

FOCACCIA WITH ROSEMARY

🍽 SERVES 6–8   🥣 WORK TIME 30–35 MINUTES*   ☕ BAKING TIME 15–20 MINUTES

EQUIPMENT

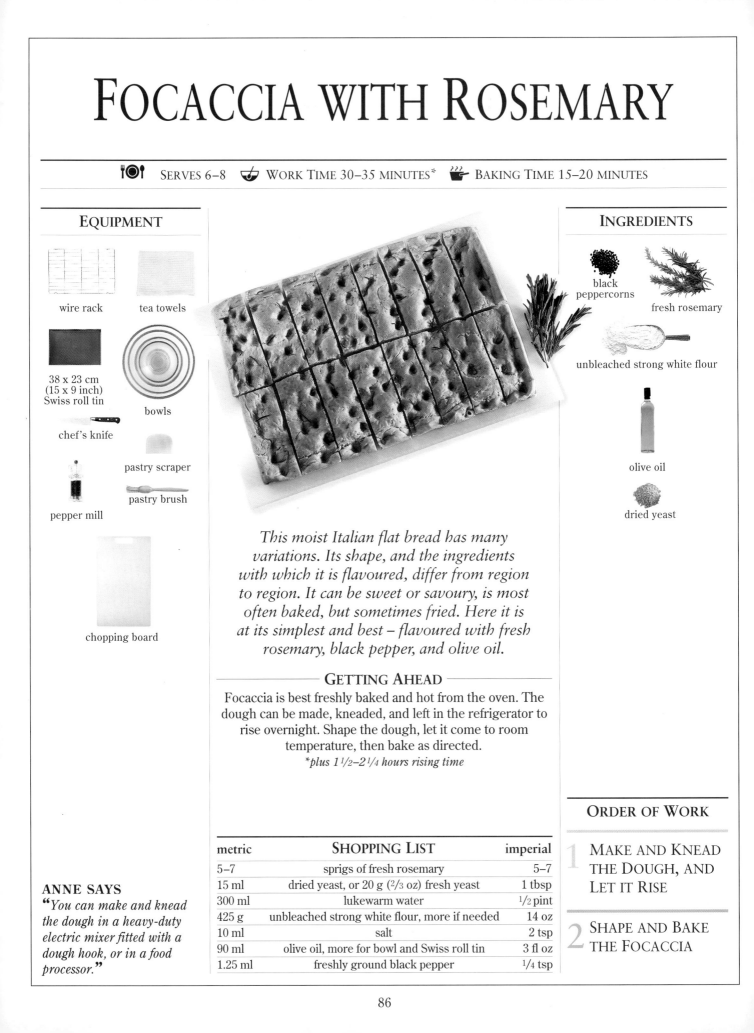

wire rack

tea towels

38 x 23 cm
(15 x 9 inch)
Swiss roll tin

bowls

chef's knife

pastry scraper

pastry brush

pepper mill

chopping board

ANNE SAYS
*"You can make and knead
the dough in a heavy-duty
electric mixer fitted with a
dough hook, or in a food
processor."*

INGREDIENTS

black
peppercorns

fresh rosemary

unbleached strong white flour

olive oil

dried yeast

*This moist Italian flat bread has many
variations. Its shape, and the ingredients
with which it is flavoured, differ from region
to region. It can be sweet or savoury, is most
often baked, but sometimes fried. Here it is
at its simplest and best – flavoured with fresh
rosemary, black pepper, and olive oil.*

GETTING AHEAD
Focaccia is best freshly baked and hot from the oven. The
dough can be made, kneaded, and left in the refrigerator to
rise overnight. Shape the dough, let it come to room
temperature, then bake as directed.
plus 1 1/2–2 1/4 hours rising time

metric	SHOPPING LIST	imperial
5–7	sprigs of fresh rosemary	5–7
15 ml	dried yeast, or 20 g (2/3 oz) fresh yeast	1 tbsp
300 ml	lukewarm water	1/2 pint
425 g	unbleached strong white flour, more if needed	14 oz
10 ml	salt	2 tsp
90 ml	olive oil, more for bowl and Swiss roll tin	3 fl oz
1.25 ml	freshly ground black pepper	1/4 tsp

ORDER OF WORK

1 MAKE AND KNEAD
THE DOUGH, AND
LET IT RISE

2 SHAPE AND BAKE
THE FOCACCIA

1 MAKE AND KNEAD THE DOUGH, AND LET IT RISE

Finely chop rosemary; leaves can be tough

1 Strip the rosemary leaves from the stalks and pile two-thirds of the leaves on the chopping board. With the chef's knife, finely chop them. Reserve the remaining whole rosemary leaves for topping the focaccia.

2 In a small bowl, sprinkle or crumble the yeast over 60 ml (4 tbsp) of the water. Let stand until dissolved, stirring once, about 5 minutes.

Liquid ingredients are combined before working in flour

Keep wall of flour intact while combining liquid ingredients

3 Put the flour onto the work surface with the salt. Make a large well in the centre and add the chopped rosemary, dissolved yeast, 60 ml (4 tbsp) of the oil, the freshly ground pepper, and the remaining water.

4 With your fingertips, work the ingredients in the well until thoroughly mixed.

5 Gradually draw in the flour with the pastry scraper and work it into the other ingredients with your hand to form a smooth dough. It should be soft and sticky.

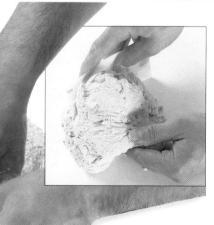

! TAKE CARE !
The dough should be quite sticky so add as little flour as possible when kneading.

6 Sprinkle the dough and your hands with flour and knead, lifting the dough up and throwing it down until it is very smooth, elastic, and forms a ball, 5–7 minutes.

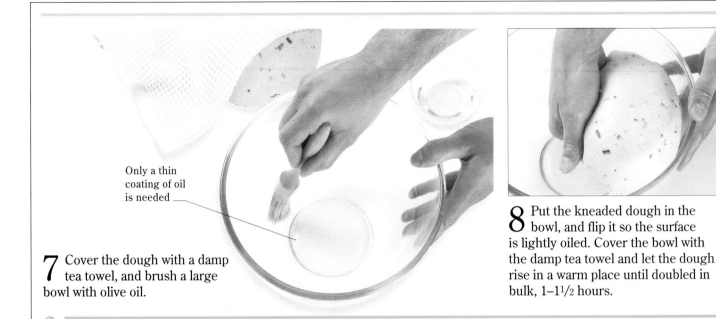

Only a thin coating of oil is needed

7 Cover the dough with a damp tea towel, and brush a large bowl with olive oil.

8 Put the kneaded dough in the bowl, and flip it so the surface is lightly oiled. Cover the bowl with the damp tea towel and let the dough rise in a warm place until doubled in bulk, 1–1½ hours.

2 SHAPE AND BAKE THE FOCACCIA

1 Once the dough has doubled in bulk, generously brush the Swiss roll tin with olive oil.

2 Turn the dough onto a lightly floured work surface and knead with your hand just to knock out the air, 15–20 seconds. Cover the dough and let rest, about 5 minutes.

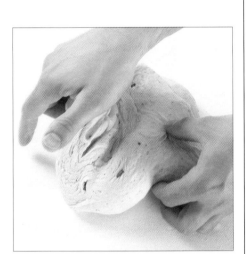

3 Transfer the dough to the tin. With your hands, flatten the dough to fill the tin evenly. Cover the dough with a dry tea towel, and let rise in a warm place until puffed, 35–45 minutes.

Rosemary is traditional focaccia garnish

4 Heat the oven to 200°C (400°F, Gas 6). Brush the dough with the remaining oil, then top with the reserved rosemary leaves.

5 With your fingertips, poke the dough all over to make deep dimples.

Press down through dough to tin to make deep dimples

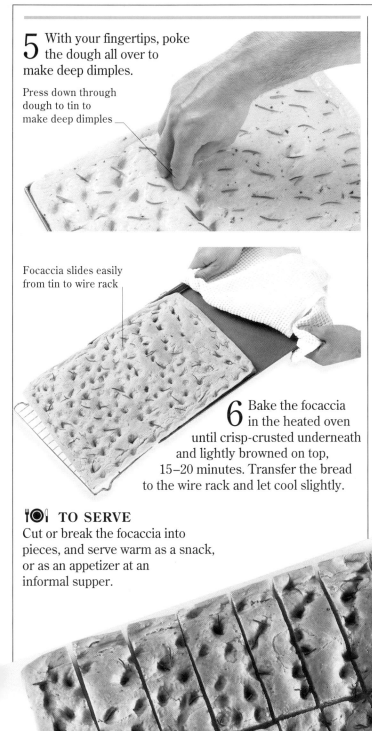

Focaccia slides easily from tin to wire rack

6 Bake the focaccia in the heated oven until crisp-crusted underneath and lightly browned on top, 15–20 minutes. Transfer the bread to the wire rack and let cool slightly.

🍽 TO SERVE
Cut or break the focaccia into pieces, and serve warm as a snack, or as an appetizer at an informal supper.

Dimples in dough hold olive oil and rosemary

FOCACCIA WITH SAGE
Here, chopped fresh sage is kneaded into the dough, which is shaped to resemble a large leaf.

1 Omit the rosemary and freshly ground black pepper. Finely chop the leaves from 3–5 sprigs of fresh sage.
2 Make the dough, adding the chopped sage to the well in place of the rosemary. Knead the dough, and let rise as directed. Brush a baking sheet with oil.
3 Knock the air out of the dough, and let rest as directed. With a rolling pin and your hands, roll and pull the dough into a 35 cm (14 inch) oval. Transfer to the baking sheet.
4 With a scalpel, make diagonal slashes through the dough to resemble the veins of a leaf, pulling the slits apart with your fingers. Let the dough rise as directed, then brush with 15 ml (1 tbsp) olive oil. Bake as directed.

ANNE SAYS
"If the slashes close while the dough rises, gently open them before baking."

CHOCOLATE BREAD

🍽 MAKES 1 LARGE LOAF   🥣 WORK TIME 35–40 MINUTES*   ♨ BAKING TIME 45–50 MINUTES

EQUIPMENT

heavy-duty electric mixer
with paddle and dough hook

1.5 litre
(2 1/3 pint)
soufflé dish   bowls

wire rack   tea towels

pastry brush

chef's knife

chopping board

ANNE SAYS
"*You will need a heavy-duty electric mixer to mix and knead dough properly. Use one with paddle and dough hook attachments.*"

From the raisins and candied orange peel in panettone *it is but a short step to chocolate. So trust an Italian baker to have thought up this delicious dessert bread, darkened with cocoa powder and chunks of chopped chocolate. Use good-quality, bittersweet chocolate for the best flavour.*

GETTING AHEAD

This bread is best on the day of baking, but can be tightly wrapped and kept 2–3 days, or it can be frozen.
plus 1 3/4–2 1/4 hours rising time

INGREDIENTS

bittersweet chocolate

cocoa powder

sugar

unbleached strong white flour

unsalted butter

dried yeast

ORDER OF WORK

1 MIX AND KNEAD THE DOUGH, AND LET IT RISE; SHAPE THE LOAF

2 BAKE THE LOAF

metric	SHOPPING LIST	imperial
12.5 ml	dried yeast, or 15 g (1/2 oz) fresh yeast	2 1/2 tsp
375 ml	lukewarm water	12 fl oz
15 ml	unsalted butter, softened, more for bowl and soufflé dish	1 tbsp
30 g	cocoa powder	1 oz
500 g	unbleached strong white flour, more if needed	1 lb
10 ml	salt	2 tsp
60 g	sugar, more for glaze	2 oz
125 g	bittersweet chocolate	4 oz

1 MIX AND KNEAD THE DOUGH, AND LET IT RISE; SHAPE THE LOAF

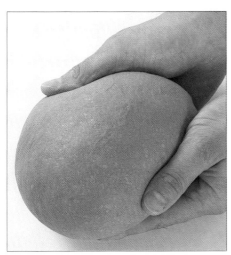

1 Mix and knead the dough in the heavy-duty electric mixer (see box, page 92).

2 Brush a large bowl with melted butter. Put the kneaded dough in the bowl, and flip it so that the surface is lightly buttered.

Turn dough against side of bowl for even coating of melted butter

Damp tea towel keeps dough moist as it rises

Dough is smooth and elastic from kneading

3 Cover the bowl with a damp tea towel and let the dough rise in a warm place until doubled in bulk, 1–1 1/2 hours.

4 Brush the soufflé dish with melted butter. Set the prepared soufflé dish aside until ready to use.

Chef's knife makes easy work of chopping chocolate

Chunks of chocolate should be coarsely chopped

5 Cut the chocolate into large chunks, then coarsely chop them with the chef's knife. Chill the chocolate.

ANNE SAYS

"*Chilling the chocolate for a few minutes prevents it from melting when kneaded into the dough.*"

HOW TO MIX AND KNEAD DOUGH IN A HEAVY-DUTY ELECTRIC MIXER

A heavy-duty electric mixer makes light work of mixing and kneading bread dough. First combine the ingredients using the paddle, then attach the dough hook to knead. This dough-making method can be used in a variety of recipes, using dry and liquid ingredients as specified.

1 In a small bowl, sprinkle or crumble the yeast over 60 ml (4 tbsp) of the water. Let stand until dissolved, stirring once, about 5 minutes.

Paddle attachment combines liquid ingredients, butter, and cocoa evenly

2 Put the dissolved yeast, softened butter, and cocoa powder into the mixer bowl. Pour in the remaining water and mix with the paddle on low speed to combine.

ANNE SAYS
"The paddle blends without aerating, producing a smooth batter, the base of an even-textured dough."

Softened butter blends easily

Flour should be completely incorporated before adding more

3 Add half of the flour to the mixer bowl with the salt and sugar, and beat with the paddle just until combined. Add the remaining flour, 60 g (2 oz) at a time, beating after each addition.

4 Keep adding flour until the dough pulls away from the side of the bowl in a ball. It should be soft and slightly sticky.

5 Attach the dough hook. On medium speed, knead the dough until it is very smooth and elastic, 3–5 minutes. If necessary, add more flour while kneading.

! TAKE CARE !
If the dough climbs up the hook, stop the machine, and push the dough back down.

6 Remove the kneaded dough from the dough hook, and shape the dough into a ball.

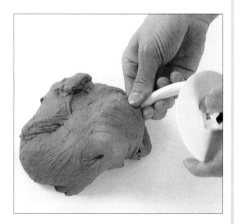

6 Once the dough has risen, turn it from the bowl onto a lightly floured work surface.

7 Knead the dough with your hand just to knock out the air, 15–20 seconds. Cover the dough, and let rest, about 5 minutes.

Dough is spongy in texture after rising

8 Knead the chopped chocolate into the dough until evenly blended, 2–3 minutes. Cover the dough, and let rest again, about 5 minutes.

ANNE SAYS
"*The chocolate is added just before shaping the loaf so that it does not inhibit the first rising.*"

Chocolate is gradually worked into dough

Pinch dough firmly to make tight seam

9 Shape the dough into a loose ball. Fold the sides over to the centre, turning and pinching to make a tight round ball.

ANNE SAYS
"*For the best flavour, it is important to use good-quality chocolate. A small amount of bittersweet chocolate, with its high proportion of cocoa solids and cocoa butter, goes a long way in baking. Flavour varies from brand to brand, so experiment to find your favourite.*"

Hands should be lightly floured to keep dough from sticking

10 Carefully put the ball of dough, seam-side down, into the prepared soufflé dish.

Dough will take on shape of soufflé dish as it rises

11 Cover the dish with a dry tea towel, and let the loaf rise in a warm place until the soufflé dish is just full, about 45 minutes.

2 BAKE THE LOAF

1 Heat the oven to 220°C (425°F, Gas 7). Brush the top of the loaf with water.

Loaf is brushed with water so sugar sticks and melts while baking

Dough rises to fill soufflé dish

2 Lightly sprinkle the top of the loaf with sugar, spreading it as evenly as possible.

Tap centre of loaf to test if bread is done

Use tea towel to handle hot bread

3 Bake the loaf in the heated oven, 20 minutes. Lower the heat to 190°C (375°F, Gas 5) and continue baking until well browned, 25–30 minutes longer. Remove the loaf from the soufflé dish. Turn it over and tap the bottom with your knuckles. The bread should sound hollow, and the sides should feel crisp when pressed.

4 Using a dry tea towel, carefully transfer the bread to the wire rack and let cool completely.

Top of bread is richly coloured

🍴 **TO SERVE**
In the Italian tradition, Chocolate Bread can be sliced and spread with a mild soft cheese such as mascarpone. Accompany with a glass of red wine, if you like.

Chocolate bread has a large, tender crumb

Pieces of **bittersweet chocolate** impart rich flavour

CHOCOLATE AND ORANGE ROLLS

Here, cocoa powder is replaced with grated orange zest and the dough is shaped into large rolls.

1 Omit the cocoa powder. Finely grate the zest of 2 oranges. Make the dough, adding the grated orange zest to the softened butter and liquid ingredients in place of the cocoa powder. Knead the dough, and let rise as directed. Chop and chill the chocolate. Brush 2 baking sheets with melted butter.
2 Knock the air out of the dough, and let it rest. Knead in the chocolate and let the dough rest again. Cut the dough in half. Roll 1 piece of dough into a cylinder about 5 cm (2 inches) in diameter. Cut the cylinder into 4 pieces. Shape and divide the remaining dough.
3 Lightly flour the work surface. Cup a piece of dough under the palm of your hand and roll the dough in a circular motion so it forms a smooth ball. Set the ball on 1 of the prepared baking sheets. Shape the remaining dough. Cover and let rise in a warm place until doubled in bulk, about 30 minutes.
4 Heat the oven to 220°C (425°F, Gas 7). Glaze the rolls as directed, and bake them in the heated oven until they begin to brown, 15 minutes. Lower the heat to 190°C (375°F, Gas 5) and bake until well browned and the rolls sound hollow when tapped, 15–20 minutes longer. Makes 8 rolls.

AUNT LOUIE'S YULE BREAD

🍽 MAKES 1 LARGE LOAF   🥣 WORK TIME 50–55 MINUTES*   🍲 BAKING TIME 60–65 MINUTES

EQUIPMENT

23 x 12 x 7.5 cm loaf tin

pastry brush

chef's knife

plastic bag

saucepan

tea towels

sieve

bowls

wire rack

chopping board

rolling pin

metal skewer

ANNE SAYS
"You can make and knead the dough in a heavy-duty electric mixer fitted with a dough hook."

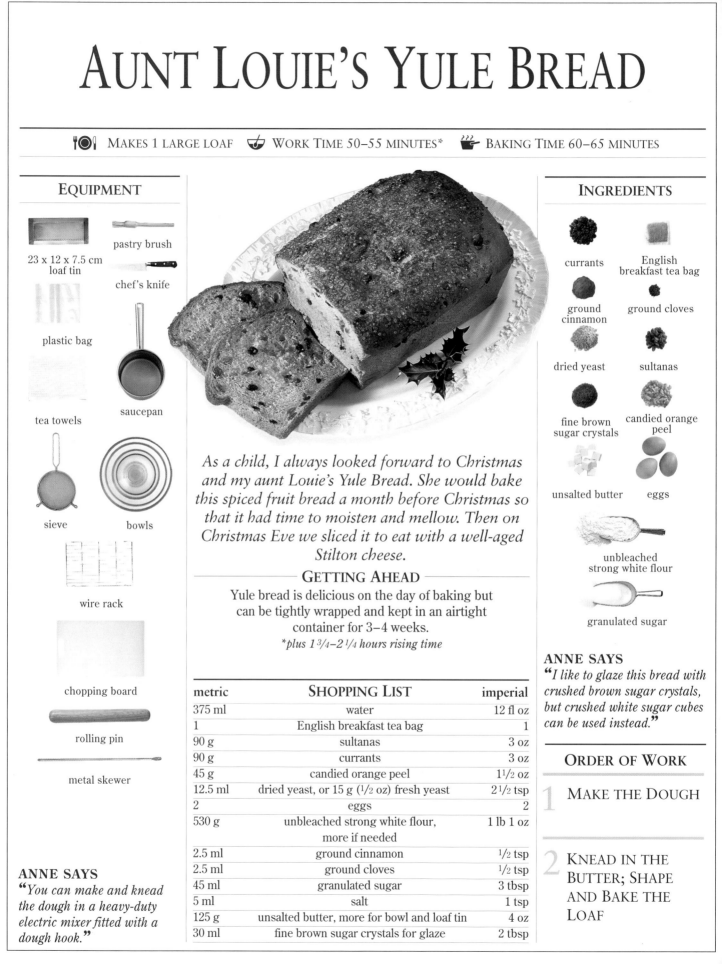

As a child, I always looked forward to Christmas and my aunt Louie's Yule Bread. She would bake this spiced fruit bread a month before Christmas so that it had time to moisten and mellow. Then on Christmas Eve we sliced it to eat with a well-aged Stilton cheese.

GETTING AHEAD

Yule bread is delicious on the day of baking but can be tightly wrapped and kept in an airtight container for 3–4 weeks.

*plus 1 3/4–2 1/4 hours rising time

metric	SHOPPING LIST	imperial
375 ml	water	12 fl oz
1	English breakfast tea bag	1
90 g	sultanas	3 oz
90 g	currants	3 oz
45 g	candied orange peel	1 1/2 oz
12.5 ml	dried yeast, or 15 g (1/2 oz) fresh yeast	2 1/2 tsp
2	eggs	2
530 g	unbleached strong white flour, more if needed	1 lb 1 oz
2.5 ml	ground cinnamon	1/2 tsp
2.5 ml	ground cloves	1/2 tsp
45 ml	granulated sugar	3 tbsp
5 ml	salt	1 tsp
125 g	unsalted butter, more for bowl and loaf tin	4 oz
30 ml	fine brown sugar crystals for glaze	2 tbsp

INGREDIENTS

currants

English breakfast tea bag

ground cinnamon

ground cloves

dried yeast

sultanas

fine brown sugar crystals

candied orange peel

unsalted butter

eggs

unbleached strong white flour

granulated sugar

ANNE SAYS
"I like to glaze this bread with crushed brown sugar crystals, but crushed white sugar cubes can be used instead."

ORDER OF WORK

1 MAKE THE DOUGH

2 KNEAD IN THE BUTTER; SHAPE AND BAKE THE LOAF

1 MAKE THE DOUGH

1 Bring 300 ml (¹/₂ pint) of the water to a boil. Take from the heat, add the tea bag, and let soak, 5 minutes. Put the sultanas and currants in a medium bowl. Discard the tea bag. Pour over the warm tea, and let the fruit soak until plump, 10–15 minutes.

Strain, reserving both fruit and tea

2 Strain the fruit, reserving the tea. Chop the candied orange peel. Set all of the fruit aside.

3 In a small bowl, sprinkle or crumble the yeast over 60 ml (4 tbsp) lukewarm water. Let stand until dissolved, stirring once, about 5 minutes.

4 In a small bowl, beat the eggs with a fork just until mixed.

For best results water should be 43°–46°C (110°–115°F)

6 Make a well in the centre and add the reserved tea, eggs, and dissolved yeast.

Dissolved yeast is smooth and frothy

Deep well holds liquid ingredients

5 Using the sieve, sift the flour, cinnamon, cloves, sugar, and salt into a large bowl.

7 With your fingertips, work the ingredients in the well until thoroughly mixed.

Hand is best tool for mixing dough

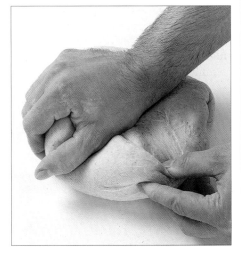

8 Gradually draw in the flour and work it into the other ingredients with your hand to form a smooth dough. It should be soft and slightly sticky.

9 Turn the dough onto a floured work surface. Sprinkle the dough and your hands with flour, and begin to knead by holding the dough with one hand and pushing it away from you with the other.

Kneading develops gluten, helping dough to rise

10 Continue to knead by peeling the dough from the surface. Give it a quarter turn and knead until it is very smooth, elastic, and forms a ball, 5–7 minutes. If the dough sticks while kneading, flour the work surface.

11 Wash the large bowl. Brush the bowl with melted butter.

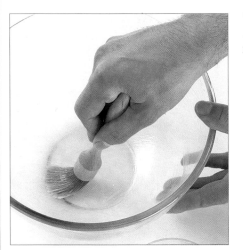

12 Put the kneaded dough in the bowl, and flip it so that the surface is lightly buttered. Cover the bowl with a damp tea towel and let the dough rise in a warm place until doubled in bulk, 1–1 1/2 hours.

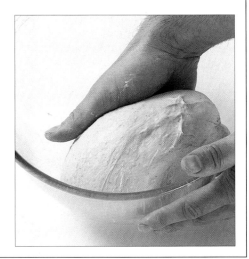

2 KNEAD IN THE BUTTER; SHAPE AND BAKE THE LOAF

1 Brush the loaf tin with melted butter. Turn the dough onto a lightly floured work surface and knead with your hand just to knock out the air, 15–20 seconds. Cover the dough, and let rest, about 5 minutes.

2 Knead in the softened butter, pinching and squeezing the dough with both hands. Knead the dough on the floured work surface until smooth again, 3–5 minutes. Cover, and let rest, about 5 minutes longer.

3 Knead the sultanas, currants, and candied orange peel into the dough until evenly blended, 2–3 minutes. Cover the dough, and let rest, about 5 minutes.

Knead in fruit by pushing and turning dough

Dough will become smooth with kneading

4 Flour your hands and pat the dough into a 25 x 20 cm (10 x 8 inch) rectangle on the floured work surface; rested dough will stretch easily.

5 Starting with a long side, roll the rectangle into a cylinder, pinching and sealing it with your fingers as you go.

ANNE SAYS
"If necessary, flour your hands while rolling dough."

Seam is pinched to form tight cylinder

Dough is coloured with spice and tea

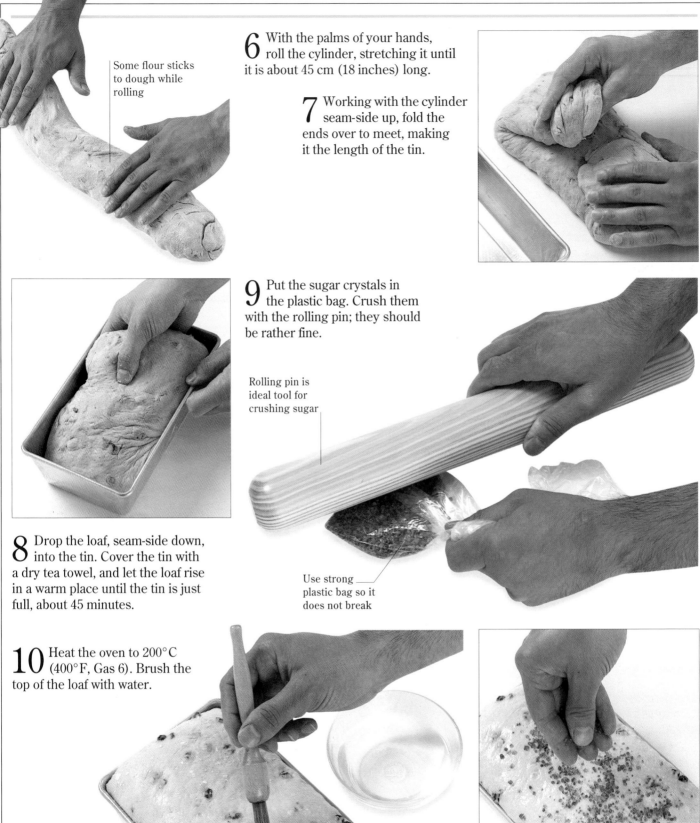

6 With the palms of your hands, roll the cylinder, stretching it until it is about 45 cm (18 inches) long.

Some flour sticks to dough while rolling

7 Working with the cylinder seam-side up, fold the ends over to meet, making it the length of the tin.

9 Put the sugar crystals in the plastic bag. Crush them with the rolling pin; they should be rather fine.

Rolling pin is ideal tool for crushing sugar

Use strong plastic bag so it does not break

8 Drop the loaf, seam-side down, into the tin. Cover the tin with a dry tea towel, and let the loaf rise in a warm place until the tin is just full, about 45 minutes.

10 Heat the oven to 200°C (400°F, Gas 6). Brush the top of the loaf with water.

Loaf is brushed with water so sugar sticks while baking

11 Sprinkle the loaf with the sugar crystals, spreading them as evenly as possible.

Metal skewer tests if bread is cooked through

12 Bake the loaf in the heated oven until it puffs and begins to brown, about 15 minutes. Lower the heat to 180°C (350°F, Gas 4) and continue baking until the metal skewer inserted in the centre comes out clean, 45–50 minutes longer.

! TAKE CARE !
If the top of the bread browns too quickly, cover it loosely with aluminium foil.

VARIATION
YORKSHIRE YULE BREAD
Whisky-soaked fruit spikes this festive bread.

13 Remove the bread from the tin. Turn it over and tap the bottom with your knuckles. The bread should sound hollow and the sides should feel crisp when pressed. Transfer the bread to the wire rack and let cool completely.

1 Omit the tea bag and sugar crystals. Soak the sultanas and currants in 60 ml (4 tbsp) whisky, stirring occasionally, 25–30 minutes. Strain the fruit, reserving the whisky. Chop the candied orange peel and set the fruit aside. Dissolve the yeast as directed.
2 Make the dough, adding the reserved whisky to the well with the dissolved yeast, 250 ml (8 fl oz) lukewarm water, and the eggs. Knead the dough, and let rise as directed.
3 Brush a 1.5 litre (2⅓ pint) charlotte mould or soufflé dish with melted butter. Knock the air out of the dough and let rest as directed. Knead in the butter and the fruit. Shape the dough into a tight round ball. Put the ball, seam-side down, into the prepared mould. Cover, and let rise as directed.
4 Heat the oven to 200°C (400°F, Gas 6). Make the egg glaze: lightly beat 1 egg with 2.5 ml (½ tsp) salt. Brush the loaf with the egg glaze. Using a small sieve, sprinkle the dough with 15 ml (1 tbsp) icing sugar.
5 Bake the loaf, 15 minutes; lower the heat to 180°C (350°F, Gas 4) and continue baking, 50–55 minutes longer. Let cool.

⅋⦿ TO SERVE
This bread is a holiday treat. It is good for breakfast, served plain or toasted and spread with butter, or it can be sliced and served with a blue-veined cheese.

Crushed sugar crystals make a crispy glaze

Tea-soaked fruit studs yule bread

OLD-FASHIONED CORNBREAD

🍽 SERVES 8 🥄 WORK TIME 15–20 MINUTES 🍲 BAKING TIME 20–25 MINUTES

EQUIPMENT

bowls

sieve

pastry brush

chef's knife

chopping board

small saucepan

23 cm (9 inch)
flameproof cast-
iron frying pan†

rubber spatula

metal skewer

wire rack

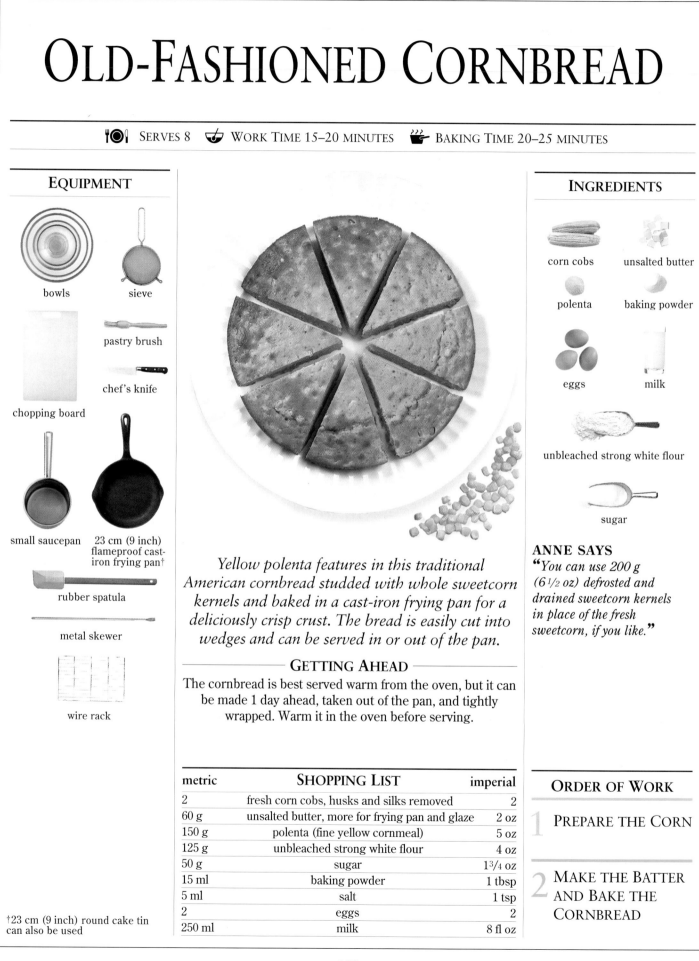

*Yellow polenta features in this traditional
American cornbread studded with whole sweetcorn
kernels and baked in a cast-iron frying pan for a
deliciously crisp crust. The bread is easily cut into
wedges and can be served in or out of the pan.*

GETTING AHEAD

The cornbread is best served warm from the oven, but it can
be made 1 day ahead, taken out of the pan, and tightly
wrapped. Warm it in the oven before serving.

INGREDIENTS

corn cobs

unsalted butter

polenta

baking powder

eggs

milk

unbleached strong white flour

sugar

ANNE SAYS
*"You can use 200 g
(6 ½ oz) defrosted and
drained sweetcorn kernels
in place of the fresh
sweetcorn, if you like."*

metric	SHOPPING LIST	imperial
2	fresh corn cobs, husks and silks removed	2
60 g	unsalted butter, more for frying pan and glaze	2 oz
150 g	polenta (fine yellow cornmeal)	5 oz
125 g	unbleached strong white flour	4 oz
50 g	sugar	1¾ oz
15 ml	baking powder	1 tbsp
5 ml	salt	1 tsp
2	eggs	2
250 ml	milk	8 fl oz

†23 cm (9 inch) round cake tin
can also be used

ORDER OF WORK

1 PREPARE THE CORN

2 MAKE THE BATTER
AND BAKE THE
CORNBREAD

1 PREPARE THE CORN

1 Heat the oven to 220°C (425°F, Gas 7). Hold 1 cob vertically and cut away the kernels from the tip down to the chopping board. Turn the cob and continue cutting, removing as many whole kernels as possible.

Hold cob firmly against chopping board when removing kernels

2 Cut the kernels away from the remaining cob. Put all the kernels into a small bowl.

3 Working over the bowl, use the back of the chef's knife to scrape each cob and remove the corn pulp.

2 MAKE THE BATTER AND BAKE THE CORNBREAD

2 Sift the polenta, flour, sugar, baking powder, and salt into a large bowl, and make a well in the centre. Add the fresh sweetcorn kernels to the well.

1 Brush the frying pan with melted butter. Melt the butter for the batter in the small saucepan.

ANNE SAYS

"Generously buttering the frying pan prevents the bread from sticking, and makes the crust crisp and golden."

Sweetcorn kernels are tender and juicy

3 In a medium bowl, whisk the eggs, melted butter, and milk until thoroughly combined.

Rubber spatula combines ingredients gently

Sweetcorn kernels are blended into batter

4 Pour three-quarters of the milk mixture into the well in the flour, and stir with the spatula.

5 Gradually draw in the dry ingredients, adding the remaining milk mixture, and stirring to make a smooth batter.

! TAKE CARE !
Do not overstir the batter or the bread will be heavy.

6 Pour the cornbread batter into the prepared frying pan and brush the top generously with melted butter.

Clean skewer means bread is properly baked

Cornbread bakes to a golden brown

7 Bake in the heated oven until the bread starts to shrink from the side of the frying pan and the metal skewer inserted in the centre comes out clean, 20–25 minutes. Let the cornbread cool slightly on the wire rack.

🍴 **TO SERVE**
Cut the cornbread into wedges and serve warm. This bread is traditionally served with spicy chilli con carne or roast meat.

VARIATION

CORN MUFFINS WITH ROASTED RED PEPPER

In the spirit of the American West, sweet red pepper is roasted to mellow its flavour, then diced and stirred into corn muffin batter. The muffins can be baked in an ordinary or cast-iron muffin tin.

1 Omit the fresh or frozen sweetcorn. Roast, peel, and seed 1 large red pepper (see box, right). Cut the pepper halves lengthways into very thin slices. Cut the slices across into small dice.

2 Heat the oven to 220°C (425°F, Gas 7). Generously brush a 12-hole muffin tin with melted butter; each hole should measure 60 ml (4 tbsp).

3 Make the cornbread batter, using only 15 ml (1 tbsp) sugar and adding the diced roasted pepper in place of the sweetcorn kernels. Spoon the batter into the muffin tin, dividing it equally among the buttered holes. Bake the muffins in the heated oven, until they start to shrink from the sides of the holes and a metal skewer inserted in the centre of a muffin comes out clean, 15–20 minutes. Unmould the muffins and let cool slightly. Makes 12 muffins.

ANNE SAYS
"If using a cast-iron muffin tin, make sure it is well seasoned. This helps prevent the muffins from sticking."

HOW TO ROAST, PEEL, AND SEED A PEPPER

Grilling a pepper makes it easy to peel and gives it a smoky flavour.

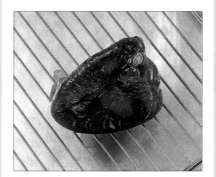

1 Heat the grill. Set the pepper on the rack 10 cm (4 inches) from the heat. Grill, turning as needed, until the skin blackens and blisters, 10–12 minutes. Immediately put the pepper in a plastic bag, close it, and let cool.

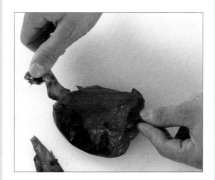

2 With a small knife, peel off the skin. Rinse the pepper under cold running water and pat dry with paper towels.

3 Cut around the core of the pepper and pull it out. Cut the pepper lengthways in half and scrape out the seeds. Cut away the white ribs on the inside.

IRISH SODA BREAD

🍴 MAKES 1 LARGE LOAF   🥄 WORK TIME 10–15 MINUTES   ☕ BAKING TIME 35–40 MINUTES

EQUIPMENT

baking sheet

bowls

pastry brush

scalpel†

sieve

INGREDIENTS

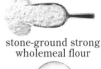

stone-ground strong wholemeal flour

buttermilk

butter

bicarbonate of soda

I first came across this wholemeal bread in southern Ireland and was surprised by its light, almost cake-like texture. Stone-ground flour makes a great difference to the flavour, and the bread takes very little time to make.

GETTING AHEAD

Irish Soda Bread is best eaten warm from the oven. Mix the ingredients and bake the bread just before serving.

ANNE SAYS

"*Stone-ground wheat flour differs from other wheat flours in that it is ground between stone instead of steel rollers. Stone rollers crush the grain slowly, without stripping away the vitamin-rich wheat germ. Steel rollers crush the grain at a much faster speed, separating the germ and producing a more finely ground flour.*"

ORDER OF WORK

1 MAKE THE DOUGH

2 SHAPE AND BAKE THE LOAF

metric	SHOPPING LIST	imperial
500 g	stone-ground strong wholemeal flour	1 lb
7.5 ml	bicarbonate of soda	1½ tsp
7.5 ml	salt	1½ tsp
500 ml	buttermilk, more if needed	16 fl oz
	butter for baking sheet	

†small knife can also be used

1 MAKE THE DOUGH

1 Heat the oven to 200°C (400°F, Gas 6). Brush the baking sheet with melted butter.

2 Sift the flour, bicarbonate of soda, and salt into a large bowl, tipping the bran from the sieve into the bowl.

Stone-ground flour is rich with wheatbran and wheatgerm

Sifting aerates flour, retaining bran

3 Mix with your hand to combine the dry ingredients, and make a well in the centre.

Well holds buttermilk

Large bowl holds ingredients easily

4 In a steady stream, pour the buttermilk into the centre of the well.

5 With your hand, quickly draw the flour into the buttermilk to make a soft dough. It should be slightly sticky. Do not overwork the dough or the bread will be heavy. Add a little more buttermilk if the dough seems dry.

2 SHAPE AND BAKE THE LOAF

1 Turn the dough onto a lightly floured work surface, and quickly shape it into a round loaf.

2 Put the loaf on the prepared baking sheet and pat it down with the palms of your hands to form a round, about 5 cm (2 inches) high. With the scalpel, make an "x", 1.25 cm (1/2 inch) deep, in the top of the loaf.

Deep slashes allow steam to escape during baking

3 Bake the loaf in the heated oven until it is brown, 35–40 minutes. Turn the loaf over and tap the bottom with your knuckles. The bread should sound hollow. Transfer the bread to the wire rack and let cool slightly.

¶⊙¶ TO SERVE

Cut the bread into slices or wedges and serve warm, with plenty of butter. Soda bread is a traditional accompaniment to soup or stew, and makes very good toast.

Cross in centre of this hearty loaf is traditional decoration

VARIATION

GRIDDLE CAKES

Irish Soda Bread is easily transformed into individual griddle cakes. Cooked on a hot griddle or heavy cast-iron frying pan, these cakes are crisp on the outside, moist in the centre, and sweetened with sugar.

1 Heat a griddle or a large cast-iron frying pan to medium-low. Make the batter: put 250 g (8 oz) stone-ground strong wholemeal flour, 7.5 ml (1 1/2 tsp) bicarbonate of soda, and 7.5 ml (1 1/2 tsp) salt into a large bowl. Stir in 90 g (3 oz) quick-cooking rolled oats with 45 ml (3 tbsp) soft brown sugar, and make a well in the centre. Pour 600 ml (1 pint) buttermilk into the well. Stir with a rubber spatula, gradually drawing in the dry ingredients to make a smooth batter.
2 Brush the heated griddle with melted butter. Using a small ladle, drop about 30 ml (2 tbsp) batter onto the hot surface. Repeat to make 5–6 cakes. Cook until the underside of the griddle cakes are golden brown and crisp, about 5 minutes. Turn them over and brown them on the other side, about 5 minutes longer. Transfer to a platter, cover, and keep warm. Continue with the remaining batter, brushing the griddle with more butter as needed. Serve the cakes warm with butter and jam. Makes 20 cakes.

ANNE SAYS
"*Seasoning your cast-iron frying pan helps prevent foods from sticking. Cover the bottom of the pan with 1.25 cm (1/2 inch) of oil and a generous handful of coarse salt, and leave it overnight. Heat it gently on the stove or in the oven until the oil is very hot and almost smoking. Leave the pan until almost tepid, then discard the oil and salt and wipe the pan dry. Once a pan has been seasoned it should never be washed, but wiped out with a cloth while still warm.*"

VARIATION

SKILLET BREAD

A combination of white and stone-ground wholemeal flours makes this variation a little lighter than traditional Irish Soda Bread. The dough is cut into wedges and cooked on top of the stove in a heavy cast-iron frying pan.

1 Heat a large cast-iron frying pan to medium-low. Make the dough: put 375 g (12 oz) stone-ground strong wholemeal flour, 125 g (4 oz) unbleached strong white flour, 7.5 ml (1 1/2 tsp) bicarbonate of soda, and 5 ml (1 tsp) salt into a large bowl, and make a well in the centre. Pour 375 ml (12 fl oz) buttermilk into the well. With your hand, quickly draw the flour into the buttermilk to make a soft dough. It should be slightly sticky.
2 Turn the dough onto a lightly floured work surface, and quickly shape it into a round loaf.
3 Pat the dough with the palms of your hands to form a round, about 5 cm (2 inches) high. With a chef's knife, cut the round into 4 wedges.
4 Brush the heated pan with melted butter. Put the dough into the pan, cover, and cook, turning the wedges frequently, until golden brown and puffed, 15–20 minutes.
Serve the bread warm, spread with soft cheese or butter. Makes 4 wedges.

DEVON SCONES

🍴 MAKES 8–10 🥣 WORK TIME 15–20 MINUTES 🍲 BAKING TIME 12–15 MINUTES

EQUIPMENT

7 cm (2¾ inch)
pastry cutter

pastry blender†

bowls

sieve

pastry brush

baking sheet

INGREDIENTS

unbleached strong white flour

unsalted butter

baking powder

buttermilk

*Homemade scones are one of
the simplest and best teatime treats.
I like to use buttermilk for its flavour and
because I find it makes the lightest scones.
Serve these scones hot, with generous toppings
of butter, jam, and clotted cream, if you like.*

GETTING AHEAD
Scones take only a few minutes to make, so combine the
ingredients and bake them just before serving.

ANNE SAYS
*"At one time, buttermilk
did in fact come from the
butter-making process–it
was the liquid leftover when
butter was churned. Today,
however, it is commercially
made. If you are unable
to find buttermilk, you can
use full-fat or semi-skimmed
milk instead."*

ORDER OF WORK

1 MAKE THE DOUGH

2 SHAPE AND BAKE
THE SCONES

metric	SHOPPING LIST	imperial
250 g	unbleached strong white flour	8 oz
10 ml	baking powder	2 tsp
2.5 ml	salt	½ tsp
60 g	unsalted butter, more for baking sheet	2 oz
175 ml	buttermilk, more if needed	6 fl oz

†2 round-bladed knives can also
be used

1 MAKE THE DOUGH

1 Heat the oven to 220°C (425°F, Gas 7). Brush the baking sheet with melted butter.

2 Sift the flour, baking powder, and salt into a medium bowl. Add the butter and cut it into small pieces using the pastry blender or 2 round-bladed knives.

Pastry blender cuts butter into flour without melting it

3 Rub the mixture with your fingertips until it forms fine crumbs, lifting and crumbling to aerate it.

4 In a slow, steady stream, pour the buttermilk into the centre of the well.

Work quickly so warmth of your hands does not melt butter

5 Quickly toss the flour mixture and buttermilk with a fork to form crumbs.

! TAKE CARE !
Do not overmix the dough or the scones will be heavy. Add a little more buttermilk if the crumbs seem dry.

Fork blends dry and liquid ingredients without overmixing them

6 Stir the mixture just until the crumbs hold together and form a dough.

2 SHAPE AND BAKE THE SCONES

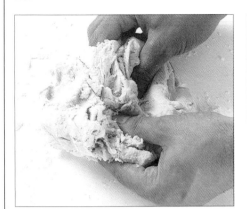

1 Turn the dough onto a floured work surface and knead lightly, 3–5 seconds.

ANNE SAYS

"Don't be tempted to make the dough smooth. The rougher the dough remains, the lighter the scones will be."

2 Pat the dough out to a round, 1.25 cm (1/2 inch) thick. Cut out rounds with the pastry cutter, patting out the trimmings and cutting additional rounds until all the dough has been used.

Cut rounds close together for greatest yield

3 Arrange the scones about 5 cm (2 inches) apart on the prepared baking sheet. Bake the scones in the heated oven until lightly browned, 12–15 minutes.

¶©¶ TO SERVE

Pile the scones in a basket and serve them hot from the oven with jam and butter.

Jam and butter make scones ideal for teatime

Homemade scones are golden on the outside, tender and flaky on the inside

CHIVE SCONES

When the quantity of buttermilk is increased, scone dough softens and can be dropped from a spoon onto the baking sheet. These made with chives are delicious – ideal for Sunday brunch.

1 Heat the oven to 220°C (425°F, Gas 7), and brush a baking sheet with melted butter. With a chef's knife, finely chop 1 small bunch of fresh chives.
2 Make the scone dough, adding the chives and 250 ml (8 fl oz) buttermilk to the well. Toss quickly with a fork to form crumbs, then stir the mixture just until it holds together. Do not overmix the dough or the scones will be heavy.

Space scones evenly, leaving them room to rise

3 With a tablespoon, drop spoonfuls of dough about 5 cm (2 inches) apart onto the prepared baking sheet. Bake as directed. Makes 10–12 scones.

CURRANT SCONES

Currants make this a fruity variation of Devon Scones. The dough is shaped into a round, and then cut into wedges. Serve the scones hot, with butter or clotted cream.

1 Heat the oven to 220°C (425°F, Gas 7), and brush a baking sheet with melted butter. Make the glaze: beat 1 egg yolk and 15 ml (1 tbsp) buttermilk to mix well, and set aside.
2 Sift the flour, baking powder, salt, 1.25 ml ($1/4$ tsp) bicarbonate of soda, and 10 ml (2 tsp) sugar into a medium bowl. Work in the butter as directed, then stir in 30 ml (2 tbsp) currants.

Finish the dough as directed.

Cut straight down through dough without dragging chef's knife

3 Transfer the dough to a floured work surface. Cut it in half and pat each half into a 15 cm (6 inch) round, about 1.25 cm ($1/2$ inch) thick. With a chef's knife, cut each round into 4 wedges. Arrange the wedges about 5 cm (2 inches) apart on the prepared baking sheet . Brush them with the glaze and bake as directed. Makes 8 scones.

ORANGE-COURGETTE BREAD

🍽 MAKES 2 MEDIUM LOAVES   🥣 WORK TIME 20–25 MINUTES   ☕ BAKING TIME 55–60 MINUTES

EQUIPMENT

lemon squeezer

bowls

two loaf tins

chef's knife

wire rack

rubber spatula

sieve

grater

metal skewer

pastry brush

chopping board

INGREDIENTS

courgettes

soft brown sugar

eggs

oranges

unbleached strong white flour

baking powder

ground cinnamon

granulated sugar

walnut pieces

vanilla essence

vegetable oil

ANNE SAYS
"Be sure to use small, firm courgettes; large courgettes contain too much water, and will make the bread soggy when baked."

In this traditional American quick bread, grated courgettes add moisture and colour to a cinnamon-spiced batter, with walnuts for hearty crunch.

GETTING AHEAD

Orange-Courgette Bread is delicious warm from the oven, but can be tightly wrapped and kept for 3–4 days. It will moisten and the flavour will mature. It can also be frozen.

metric	SHOPPING LIST	imperial
375 g	courgettes	12 oz
125 g	walnut pieces	4 oz
2	oranges	2
375 g	unbleached strong white flour, more for loaf tins	12 oz
10 ml	baking powder	2 tsp
10 ml	ground cinnamon	2 tsp
5 ml	salt	1 tsp
3	eggs	3
125 ml	vegetable oil	4 fl oz
200 g	granulated sugar	6 1/2 oz
100 g	soft brown sugar	3 1/4 oz
10 ml	vanilla essence	2 tsp
	butter for loaf tins	

ORDER OF WORK

1   PREPARE THE INGREDIENTS

2   MAKE THE BATTER; BAKE THE BREAD

1 PREPARE THE INGREDIENTS

1 Heat the oven to 180°C (350°F, Gas 4). Brush two 20x10x5 cm (8x4x2 inch) loaf tins with melted butter. Sprinkle 30–45 ml (2–3 tbsp) flour in 1 of the tins and turn it to coat the bottom and sides evenly; turn the tin upside down and tap to remove excess flour. Repeat for the second tin.

2 Trim the courgettes, but do not peel them, and grate on the coarse grid of the grater.

Keep courgette at 45° angle for quick grating

3 With the chef's knife, coarsely chop the walnuts. Use your knuckles to guide the knife.

4 Finely grate the zest from the oranges. Halve 1 of the oranges and squeeze the juice; there should be about 75 ml (2 1/2 fl oz).

5 Sift the flour, baking powder, cinnamon, and salt into a large bowl. Mix in the walnuts, and make a well in the centre.

2 MAKE THE BATTER; BAKE THE BREAD

1 In a medium bowl, beat the eggs just until mixed. Add the courgettes, orange zest, oil, granulated and brown sugars, vanilla, and orange juice. Stir until thoroughly combined.

Eggs are beaten first so they mix evenly into batter

2 Pour three-quarters of the courgette mixture into the well in the flour, and stir with the spatula.

Use rubber spatula
so ingredients are
blended gently

3 Gradually draw in
the dry ingredients,
adding the remaining
courgette mixture,
and stirring to make
a smooth batter.

! TAKE CARE !
Do not overstir the batter or the
bread will be heavy.

4 Spoon the batter into the prepared
loaf tins, dividing it equally. The
tins should be about half full.

5 Bake the loaves in the heated oven
until they start to shrink from the
sides of the tins and the metal skewer
inserted in the centre comes out clean,
55–60 minutes. Let the loaves cool
slightly, then transfer from the mould
to the wire rack to cool completely.

Walnuts
add crunch
to texture
of bread

🍴 **TO SERVE**
Serve the courgette bread sliced and
spread with cream cheese for a
delicious snack. It can also be toasted
and buttered for breakfast or tea.

V A R I A T I O N
PUMPKIN BREAD

Quick bread made with pumpkin purée is another American favourite. Here, ground nutmeg and cloves are added to spice the batter.

1 Omit the courgettes and oranges. Heat the oven to 180°C (350°F, Gas 4), and prepare two 20 x 10 x 5 cm (8 x 4 x 2 inch) loaf tins as directed.
2 Prepare the batter, using 375 ml (12 fl oz) canned pumpkin purée in place of the grated courgettes, and adding 2.5 ml (1/2 tsp) ground nutmeg and 1.25 ml (1/4 tsp) ground cloves with the cinnamon.
3 Spoon the batter into the prepared tins and bake until the loaves start to shrink from the sides of the tins and a metal skewer inserted in the centre comes out clean, 55–60 minutes. Let cool as directed.

ANNE SAYS
"*Fresh pumpkin can also be used. Scrape away the seeds and fibrous threads from a 1 kg (2 lb) piece of pumpkin. Cut the pumpkin skin and flesh into chunks and put them in a large saucepan. Pour in enough water to come one-quarter of the way up the pumpkin, cover, and simmer until the flesh is tender, 25–30 minutes. Drain the pumpkin, scrape the flesh from the skin, and purée it.*"

V A R I A T I O N
BANANA BREAD

A mash of ripe bananas is delicious baked in quick bread. Spices and nuts add flavour and crunch.

1 Omit the courgettes and oranges. Heat the oven to 180°C (350°F, Gas 4). Butter and flour four 13 x 7.5 x 5 cm (5 x 3 x 2 inch) loaf tins. Finely grate the zest of 1 lemon.
2 Peel 3 ripe medium bananas and cut them into thirds. In a shallow dish, mash the bananas with a fork to form a smooth paste; there should be 375 ml (12 fl oz) mashed banana. Prepare the batter, using the mashed banana in place of the grated courgettes, and adding the lemon zest in place of the orange zest.
3 Spoon the batter into the prepared tins and bake until the loaves start to shrink from the sides of the tins and a metal skewer inserted in the centre comes out clean, 35–40 minutes. Let cool as directed.

LEMON-BLUEBERRY MUFFINS

🍴 MAKES 12   🥄 WORK TIME 20–25 MINUTES   🍲 BAKING TIME 15–20 MINUTES

EQUIPMENT

12-hole muffin tin

pastry brush   small saucepan

lemon squeezer   wire rack

sieve   grater

bowls

rubber spatula

metal skewer

ANNE SAYS
*"Each muffin hole should
measure 60 ml (4 tbsp)."*

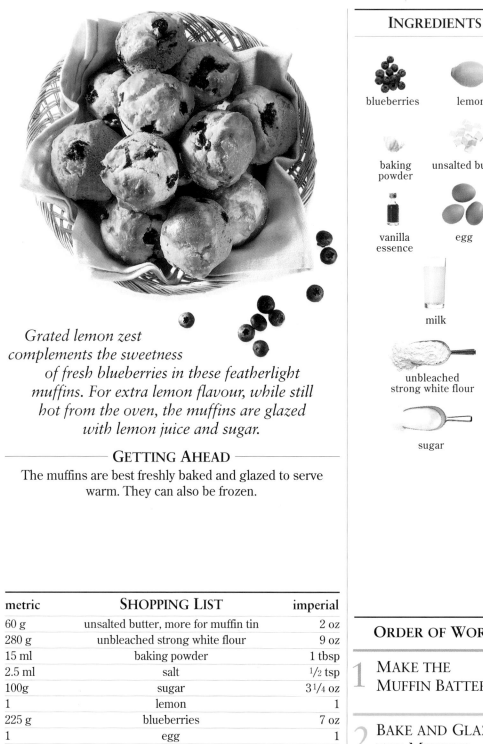

*Grated lemon zest
complements the sweetness
of fresh blueberries in these featherlight
muffins. For extra lemon flavour, while still
hot from the oven, the muffins are glazed
with lemon juice and sugar.*

GETTING AHEAD

The muffins are best freshly baked and glazed to serve
warm. They can also be frozen.

INGREDIENTS

blueberries   lemon

baking
powder   unsalted butter

vanilla
essence   egg

milk

unbleached
strong white flour

sugar

metric	SHOPPING LIST	imperial
60 g	unsalted butter, more for muffin tin	2 oz
280 g	unbleached strong white flour	9 oz
15 ml	baking powder	1 tbsp
2.5 ml	salt	1/2 tsp
100g	sugar	3 1/4 oz
1	lemon	1
225 g	blueberries	7 oz
1	egg	1
5 ml	vanilla essence	1 tsp
250 ml	milk	8 fl oz

ORDER OF WORK

1 MAKE THE
  MUFFIN BATTER

2 BAKE AND GLAZE
  THE MUFFINS

1 MAKE THE MUFFIN BATTER

1 Heat the oven to 220°C (425°F, Gas 7). Brush the muffin holes with melted butter. Melt the butter for the batter in the saucepan.

Melted butter prevents muffins from sticking

2 Using the sieve, sift the strong white flour, baking powder, and salt into a large bowl.

3 Set 30 ml (2 tbsp) sugar aside for the glaze and stir the remaining sugar into the flour. Make a well in the centre.

4 Finely grate the zest from the lemon, leaving the bitter white pith on the lemon.

Lemon zest is yellow part of peel, not bitter white pith

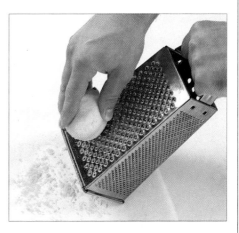

5 Halve the lemon and squeeze the juice and reserve. Pick over the blueberries, washing them only if they are dirty.

Blueberries should be plump and sweet

Press firmly on lemon to extract as much juice as possible

6 In a medium bowl, beat the egg just until mixed. Add the melted butter, lemon zest, vanilla, and milk and beat until foamy, about 1 minute.

7 In a slow, steady stream, pour the egg mixture into the well in the flour.

Liquid ingredients are mixed together before being added to flour

9 Gently fold in the blueberries, taking care not to bruise them.

! TAKE CARE !

Mix the batter just until the blueberries are evenly incorporated. Overmixing will toughen the texture of the muffins.

Gentle folding keeps colour of blueberries from running

Scoop batter and turn bowl to incorporate berries

8 Stir with the rubber spatula, gradually drawing in the dry ingredients to make a smooth batter.

2 BAKE AND GLAZE THE MUFFINS

Muffin holes are filled almost to the top

1 Spoon the batter into the muffin tin, dividing it equally among the buttered holes.

2 Bake the muffins in the heated oven until they start to shrink from the sides of the holes and the metal skewer inserted in the centre of a muffin comes out clean, 15–20 minutes. Let the muffins cool slightly on the wire rack.

3 Make the glaze: in a small bowl, stir the reserved sugar with the reserved lemon juice.

Characteristic peak in middle of muffin develops from high temperature baking

4 Remove the muffins from the tin while they are still warm. Dip the crown of a muffin into the sugar and lemon mixture and set the muffin upright on the wire rack to continue cooling. Repeat with the remaining muffins.

🍽 TO SERVE
Serve the glazed muffins while still warm.

Tart lemon glaze complements sweet, plump blueberries

LEMON-POPPY SEED MUFFINS

Lemon zest and juice are stirred into the batter for these muffins to give more of a lemon flavour, with poppy seeds adding crunch.

1 Omit the blueberries. Heat the oven to 220°C (425°F, Gas 7), and brush 9 of the muffin holes with melted butter. Melt the butter for the batter as directed. Grate the zest from the lemon and squeeze the juice.

2 Sift the flour, baking powder, and salt into a large bowl. Stir in all of the sugar. In a medium bowl, beat the egg just until mixed. Add the melted butter, vanilla, and milk, and whisk as directed. Stir in 30 ml (2 tbsp) poppy seeds, then add the lemon zest with the lemon juice. The milk may separate slightly, but this will not affect the finished muffins.

3 Combine the ingredients as directed, and spoon the mixture into the muffin tin, dividing it equally among the buttered holes. Sprinkle the muffins with 10 ml (2 tsp) sugar and bake as directed. Makes 9 muffins.

BREADS KNOW-HOW

INGREDIENTS

It does not take much to make a loaf of bread. The simplest of loaves are made of flour, yeast, water, and salt. You will find ingredients break down into three main categories: flours, leavening agents, both yeast and chemical leaveners, and other ingredients ranging from sugar and spices to buttermilk, polenta, fruit, and herbs. Remember to use only the best and freshest ingredients available.

FLOURS

Flour is the foundation of all breads. It can be made from a wide range of finely ground dried grains, seeds, and even roots and tubers, but wheat flour is by far the most common. A wheat kernel has three parts – the bran, the germ, and the endosperm. For white flour, the wheat bran and germ are removed, leaving a refined flour made up of mostly starch and protein. For bread making, the protein content of a flour is the most important characteristic. When dough is kneaded, the string-like proteins in the flour develop gluten, giving the dough its elasticity and structure, a fine mesh in which gas bubbles produced by the yeast are trapped.

The protein content of flour depends on the variety of wheat and the climate in which it is grown. Flour ground from hard-grain wheat has a relatively high protein content and develops strong gluten, while flour ground from soft-grained varieties has more starch and less gluten, desirable for pastries and cakes. Strong white flour, whether bleached or unbleached, is a combination of hard and soft flours. As flour ages, its flavour develops and it makes for better baking. Bleached flour has chemicals added to keep it white and speed ageing, while unbleached flour is left to mature naturally. Bread flour has a higher protein content and, as its name implies, is good for bread and pasta. Overall, I prefer using unbleached stong white flour for bread and have done so in these recipes. It is widely available, and is a little more versatile than bread flour.

Wholemeal flour is ground from the entire wheat kernel, so it retains all of its natural flavours and nutrients and adds a chewy texture to many breads. Despite the high protein content, wholemeal flour is more difficult to use than strong white flour. Because the bran inhibits the effectiveness of the gluten, I often mix the two, as in Wholemeal Bread. Rye flour is ground from the husked rye grain. The flour has little gluten and for a well-risen loaf it must be blended with some strong white flour. Other flours, such as buckwheat, have no gluten at all and must be mixed with generous amounts of wheat flour when yeast is used as the leavening agent.

LEAVENING AGENTS

Yeast is the standard leavening agent for bread. It is available dried and fresh, and is activated when dissolved in a warm liquid, usually water. The yeast transforms the natural sugars in flour into tiny bubbles of carbon dioxide, causing the dough to rise. As dried yeast is universally available, I have suggested its use in this book. Fresh yeast is also easy to find – if you wish to substitute it for dried yeast, use double the weight, and dissolve and mix it in exactly the same way. Easy-blend is a special variant of dried yeast. It is mixed differently, and should not be substituted directly for dried yeast.

Chemical leaveners, such as bicarbonate of soda and baking powder, are also frequently used to leaven bread. They are suited to quick breads with thinner doughs, or batters that lack sufficient gluten to contain the carbon dioxide generated by yeast. Chemical leaveners begin to work as soon as they are mixed with liquid, so these breads should be assembled and baked as quickly as possible.

OTHER BREAD INGREDIENTS

Flour may be the basic ingredient, but many other elements are involved in creating a delicious loaf. Coarse grains, such as polenta, bulghur, wheat bran, wheat germ, nuts, and seeds, are often combined with the flour to contribute both texture and flavour. Sweeteners, such as honey, granulated sugar, or soft brown sugar, help to develop the flavour of a dough or batter. In yeast doughs, sweeteners serve a dual purpose because they also increase the fermentation of the yeast. Salt is indispensable for emphasizing the flavour of plain bread, and dough made without it will have a flat, empty taste.

When fat is added to dough, it softens the texture of the finished loaf and improves its keeping qualities. Butter is a favourite choice, and in some breads, such as Rich Brioche and Kugelhopf with Walnuts, Bacon, and Herbs, it is added in generous quantities. I prefer unsalted butter because its flavour is superior. Vegetable oil is commonly used, and a liberal measure of olive oil contributes moistness as well as flavour in breads like Focaccia with Rosemary. Eggs, particularly egg yolks, add both richness and colour to breads, helping them toast well – Challah is an example.

Some loaves, such as the French Baguette, contain no fat or egg at all and are best eaten within a few hours of baking.

All of these ingredients must be mixed with liquid to make dough. Water is a neutral choice, while milk softens and whitens the texture of the bread, as in Onion and Walnut Crown. Buttermilk gives a subtle tang to yeast breads as well as quick breads, and fruit juice can add natural sweetness. Tea, potato cooking liquid, and even lager are all possible ingredients, each contributing a particular quality to the bread.

Any number of fillings, sweet or savoury, may be kneaded, rolled, or stirred into a risen dough or batter. During the holiday season, I enjoy serving Yorkshire Yule Bread, packed with currants, sultanas, and candied orange peel. Bananas and blueberries impart natural sweetness to quick breads, and in the summer months we bake our surplus garden courgettes into Orange-Courgette Bread. Sautéed onions, chopped garlic, sweetcorn, or a roasted red pepper are other favourite additions. The flavour of fresh herbs, whether chopped or puréed as in pesto, can permeate an entire loaf of bread, and you will find a variety of cheeses, including Brie, ricotta, mozzarella, and Parmesan, makes its way into the breads in this book.

TECHNIQUES

The bread making process may seem complicated, but in fact the procedure is simple enough. Whether making a yeast-leavened bread or a quick bread, there are a number of techniques on which you can rely.

YEAST BREADS

Once you have mastered a few basic techniques for making yeast breads, you can apply them to virtually every loaf you bake. You will learn how to dissolve yeast in just the right temperature of water so that it grows and works to full advantage. You will see how to make dough both in a bowl and directly on a work surface. Usually the dough is completed in one sequence, but in Split-Top White Bread, as a preliminary step, the dissolved yeast is mixed with a little flour to make a sponge, improving the flavour and texture of the bread. I will also show you how to knead dough, as well as how to let it rise. Detailed instructions on shaping loaves are also included.

When making yeast dough, I never give an exact quantity of flour because the amount can vary significantly. Not only does flour differ from mill to mill and brand to brand, but it also changes with age and humidity of storage. Therefore, I advise adding flour gradually to dough, stirring after each addition. The dough is ready to knead when it is soft and slightly sticky – more flour will be worked in during the kneading process. Note also that yeast feeds on sugar, so it will work faster when in contact with sweet ingredients. Salt, however, slows its growth, so is always mixed with other ingredients – never let salt come in direct contact with the yeast itself.

Kneading is the most important technique when making a yeast-leavened loaf, because it develops the elasticity of the dough. It also creates the structure that holds the gases produced by the yeast and supports the dough as it rises. You will need a forceful hand to push and turn a firm dough on the work surface until it is smooth and elastic. With softer doughs, such as Small Brioches and Focaccia with Rosemary, slapping and throwing is more effective.

Rising is the next step in the process of making yeast bread. Dough should be left to rise, or prove, in a warm, humid, draught-free place. The optimum temperature is around 30°C (85°F). I often leave dough to rise in the oven heated just by the gas pilot. For an electric oven, heat the oven for about 10 seconds and switch it off. The top of a warm radiator or a rack set over a gently steaming pan on the stove are other alternatives, but be sure the bowl does not get too hot. Dough can also be left to rise in the refrigerator for convenience. The cold will slow down the activity of the yeast, so rising may take 5 hours or overnight. Be sure the top of the bowl is covered with a damp cloth or a tight seal of cling film to keep the dough moist. Similarly, once shaped, some doughs can be left to rise in the refrigerator overnight. Let them come to room temperature before baking. Small rolls can be shaped and frozen up to 1 month. Let them thaw before baking.

Knowing when dough has risen sufficiently and the gluten has stretched to maximum capacity is the key to a successful loaf. In general, dough should double in bulk, and when you press a finger deep into the dough the impression will remain – if the dough springs back, it is not ready. You will see what to look for and how to test the dough in detailed "how-to" boxes.

A loaf of bread is recognizable by its shape. You will learn how to roll dough for French Baguette into long sticks, how to make Small Brioches so their "heads" do not slip to the side during baking, and how to twist egg-enriched dough into a variety of ornamental rolls. Rustic loaves of Sourdough Bread are left to rise in floured cloth-lined bowls so the soft dough holds its shape. Focaccia with Sage is slit into a distinctive leaf shape, and Challah is plaited into a characteristic four-strand tress.

123

Just before baking, the top of a loaf is often glazed and sometimes slashed. You will learn how to glaze doughs so that the finished loaves are shiny or golden, soft or crisp, as the case may be. Slashing allows the dough to expand in a neat design without cracking – the deeper the cuts, the more the bread will open to reveal the crumb. I will show you a variety of methods, some practical, like the diagonal slashes made to release steam as Seeded Rye Bread bakes, and some decorative, such as the hedgehog finish given to Orange Juice Breakfast Bread.

QUICK BREADS

As their name implies, quick breads are a complete contrast to yeast-leavened breads. These recipes can and should be made in just a few minutes, and include muffins and scones as well as larger loaves with a characteristic soft, crumbly texture, such as Orange-Courgette Bread and Old-Fashioned Cornbread. You will see how to combine the wet and dry ingredients to make a dough that is sticky and rough in appearance – sometimes it is thin enough to be a pourable batter. In complete contrast to yeast bread techniques, quick and gentle mixing is vital so that elasticity is not developed in the flour, and the finished bread remains light and airy.

As with other volumes in the *Look & Cook* series, I have also included techniques for the other ingredients that are used in these bread recipes. For instance, you will find out how to chop an onion, how to herbs, how to roast, peel, and seed a pepper, and how to peel, seed, and chop tomatoes.

CHOOSING BREADS

You will find there is a bread to accompany almost every meal. When choosing a recipe, think about the whole menu, its flavour and feel. For casual suppers of soups and stews, serve crusty loaves like Wheat Ear Baguette, Sourdough Bread, or quick and easy

Irish Soda Bread if you are short of time. Devon Scones are delicious with a traditional cream tea.

For formal dinners, delicate Dinner Rolls served warm with a pat of butter are in order. And for a very special breakfast in bed, Chocolate and Orange Rolls served with mascarpone cheese, fresh fruit, and steaming coffee are the ultimate indulgence.

Pizza and stuffed breads make fine lunch and dinner fare. Just add a crispy green salad, and Chicago Deep-Dish Pizza with its flavourful and hearty topping is perfect for a relaxed evening meal. Try Pesto Garland Bread with simply prepared pasta. Serve Spiced Lamb Pies for lunch with a yogurt and cucumber salad. Easy!

STORING BREADS

All yeast breads are best eaten on the day of baking, and some, like Potato-Chive Monkey Bread and Focaccia with Rosemary, are particularly good when still warm. Red Onion Confit and Gorgonzola Pizzas, of course, should be eaten hot from the oven. Nonetheless, many breads can be stored for up to 2 days, and some even longer if they contain a high proportion of fat. However, French Baguette, which has no fat at all, becomes stale within a few hours. Once the loaves are thoroughly cool, wrap them tightly in cling film or aluminium foil. If stored in the refrigerator, loaves will last longer, and if frozen they can usually be kept for several months.

Storage time for quick breads depends very much on their richness: plain breads like Devon Scones and Lemon-Poppy Seed Muffins are best eaten at once, while still warm. However, breads with good quantities of eggs, sugar, and, most importantly, fat, fruit, or nuts, can be kept in an airtight container for 1 week or more. Banana Bread is a good example.

To restore freshness to day-old yeast bread, wrap it loosely in a brown paper bag and put it in a warm oven until heated through, 5–10 minutes. Do not throw stale bread away, but grind it into fresh breadcrumbs in a food processor or blender, or slice or cut it into cubes to make golden croûtons.

BREADS AND YOUR HEALTH

Complex carbohydrates are often emphasized as an integral part of a healthy diet, so we are encouraged to eat a variety of whole grains, pasta, and breads. In addition to being sources of energy, they provide vitamins, minerals, and fibre.

In bread making, as in all other kinds of cooking, it is important to start with the best and freshest ingredients possible. In many parts of the country, you can find organic flours, some locally milled. For flavour and freshness, the availability of these flours is worth investigating. Check your health or whole food shop.

In a strict sense, the simpler the bread the better it is for you. Obviously, breads made without added fat are the best of all. It is important to note, however, that once spread with butter and jam, even the simplest bread loses some of its virtue. Good bread has plenty of flavour and is quite delicious if served unadorned. French Baguette and Sourdough Bread are two such examples.

Most breads do contain some fat – a little milk, olive oil, or vegetable oil. Pita, Sesame Breadsticks, and Irish Soda Bread fall into this category, while others are made with quite a lot of butter and eggs – Small Brioches, Kugelhopf with Walnuts, Bacon, and Herbs, and Yorkshire Yule Bread, to name a few. There is plenty of room for all of these breads in a healthy diet. Choose them wisely. Moderation, as always, is the key.

Remember that we do not live by bread alone. Bread and its dietary value do not stand in isolation. Consider the meal as a whole. Seek balance – enjoy fruits, vegetables, proteins, as well as bread.

HOW-TO BOXES

*In each of the recipes in **Classic Breads** you will find pictures of all the techniques used. However, some basic preparations appear in a number of recipes and these are shown in extra detail in these special "how-to" boxes:*

MICROWAVE

When making bread, the microwave can be helpful in preparing certain basic ingredients. You can melt butter, as well as heat milk and water. Be sure to follow the manufacturer's instructions for cooking speeds and times.

For yeast breads, the microwave is sometimes used to speed the rising process, but recipes need to be adapted for its use. The breads in this volume have been developed using traditional techniques, and are best suited to the bread-making methods specified in each recipe.

INDEX

ACKNOWLEDGMENTS

Photographers' Assistants Nick Allen and Sid Sideris

Chef Eric Treuille
Home Economist Maddalena Bastianelli

Typesetting Rowena Feeny and Axis Design

Text film by Disc to Print (UK) Limited

Production Consultant Lorraine Baird

Carroll & Brown Limited
would like to thank Robot Coupe (UK) Limited
who supplied the KitchenAid mixer, Magimix (UK) Limited
who supplied the Cuisine Systeme food processor, and ICTC
(0603 488-019) for supplying the Cuisinox Elysee pans
used throughout the book.

Anne Willan would like to thank her chief editor
Jacqueline Bobrow and associate editor Valerie Cipollone
for their vital help with writing this book and researching
and testing the recipes, aided by Karen Ryan and
La Varenne's chefs and trainees.

NOTES

• Metric and imperial measures have been calculated separately. Only use one set of measures as they are not exact equivalents.

• All spoon measurements are level.

• Spoon measurements are calculated using a standard 5 ml teaspoon and 15 ml tablespoon to give an accurate measurement of small amounts.